Job Search

The Insider Career Guides is a dynamic series of books which together form the ultimate career companion.

Whether looking for that first job, or hoping to develop your current career, each title in the series offers practical advice and real-life insights to put you on the inside track to success.

Other titles in the series:

Career Networking
Brian Sutton

Interviews & Assessments
Brian Sutton

Job Search

Finding jobs and securing interviews

by

Brian Sutton

First published in 2000 by
The Industrial Society
Robert Hyde House
48 Bryanston Square
London W1H 2EA

© The Industrial Society 2000

ISBN 1 85835 815 9   WX420
                      Job Application

British Library Cataloguing-in-Publication Data.
A catalogue record for this book is available from the
British Library.

Typeset by: The Midlands Book Typesetting Company
Printed by: Cromwell Press
Cover by: Sign Design
Cover image by: Don Bonsey/Tony Stone Images

The Industrial Society is a Registered Charity No. 290003

CONTENTS

ACKNOWLEDGEMENTS

Special thanks to Susannah Lear, my commissioning editor at The Industrial Society, for offering me the opportunity to write all three books in this important career series. Thank you also to those who have provided me with views and opinions to include in the books. Finally, a special note of appreciation to my wife Jacquey for her continuing support and patience.

INTRODUCTION

Careers have been described as the lifetime experience of individuals and as pathways through occupations and organisations. However, the reality is that the world of work is changing to match the needs of organisations that are themselves buffeted by changes in technology, mergers, acquisitions, take-overs, legislation, the economy and by a rise in customer expectations or increased competition.

So, if you're keen to make a success of your career, what are the important issues to be learned from these changes? Career experts generally agree that you are likely to change your employer much more frequently and may have to retrain three or four times in the course of your career. Coping with these changes is demanding, but if you're prepared to take responsibility for your own career management, including your self-development, you'll be ready to meet the challenge.

Change requires change, but the good news is that the job is alive and well, with economic reviews[1] revealing that the working population continues to grow and that more jobs are being created. Employers are keen to select the right candidates who will underpin the future profitability of the organisation. In turn, this has brought about changes to the job market, as employers are using far more innovative and less costly ways of recruiting staff than the traditional newspaper advertisement. As a result, job search has never been more demanding than it is today.

What then are the skills needed in your quest for a first or next job? Of course, having the necessary skills and

---

[1] *Review of the Economy and Employment: Labour Market Assessment,* Institute of Employment Research, March 1998.

experience that the employer is seeking is important, but you must also be able to present them properly. You'll need to understand how today's job market works and learn to combine this with effective job-search skills. Preparing for interviews and appreciating the range of selection methods used by employers should also be high on your skill list. In a competitive environment, your social skills and, in particular, your ability to market yourself energetically are vital. And in this constantly changing world, networking has become an essential survival skill.

Job Search is the first of a new series of insider guides for those who want to achieve career and job-search success in a changing workplace. The other two essential books in this series are *Career Networking* and *Interviews & Assessments*.

This book provides all the advice and guidance you'll need for successful job search, whether you are:

- a graduate or school-leaver looking for your first job
- planning your next career move
- returning to work after bringing up your family, or
- unemployed following redundancy.

Job search is about locating jobs and winning interviews. Consequently, the first chapter of this book examines employment trends and the skills that are in demand, vital information for anyone contemplating job search.

Chapter 2 reveals how employers prepare to recruit, how they describe the jobs and skills they need, and how these descriptions are used in the recruitment process. The aim here is to help you achieve a better match between your skills and personal strengths and the employer's job requirements.

Chapter 3 deals with self-assessment. Understanding your skills, personal strengths and weaknesses and developing clear career goals that reflect an understanding of what you are looking for in a job and what you have to offer employers is the foundation on which successful job search is built.

Chapter 4 shows you how to research the job market

to identify employers and jobs that are a good match for you and your needs.

Current trends in CV preparation are reviewed in Chapter 5, including tips on content and presentation.

Chapter 6 explains the principles of good time management.

In Chapter 7 we explore the visible or advertised job market, taking a look at both traditional newspaper advertising and more innovative methods such as the Internet, how you should reply to advertisements using CVs and covering letters. This is followed, in Chapter 8, by an examination of the opportunities available in the hidden job market. Chapter 9 summarises the benefits of mastering each step of the job-search process.

With checklists, case studies, quotes from employers and recruitment specialists, and 'myth busters' that challenge commonly held beliefs, this book should provide all the practical help and support you need for a targeted and successful job search. Read in conjunction with the other two books in this series, *Career Networking* and *Interviews & Assessments*, you will have the complete guide to career and job-search success.

The changing world of work

HOW ORGANISATIONS ARE CHANGING

If you asked the working members of your family and friends to tell you whether anything out of the ordinary had happened in their workplace during the last few years, you would almost certainly be told 'there has been a lot of change'. The pace of change is on the increase. Once, stability was the password for success in business. Today, however, it is not stable organisations that prosper but those that respond quickly and bring about whatever change is necessary for their continued survival.

All organisations are, to a greater or lesser degree, in a continual state of change. To survive and prosper, businesses have to grow. They must constantly come up with new ideas, develop new products, expand into new markets, reorganise, introduce new technology, and change working methods and practices. During the research for this book, employees from a variety of jobs and industries were asked what sort of change they had experienced in their particular workplace. Here are their responses:

'Managers have taken on tasks previously carried out by their secretaries.'

Office supervisor – insurance company

'Information technology is doing jobs once undertaken by employees.'

Shop-floor technician – automobile manufacturer

'Some of our employees now work from home.'

Area manager – computer manufacturer

'Customers expect lower prices and better service.'

Sales co-ordinator – road haulage company

'Some of our work has been given to an outside supplier.'
Engineer – textile goods manufacturer

'There is far more emphasis on teamwork.'
Advertising services clerk – local newspaper

'Our customers' needs and expectations affect everything we do. We are now a business driven by the business needs of our market.'
Shop manager – mobile phone supplier

'External and internal communication is much more important.'
Personnel officer – financial institution

These changes reflect the response by employers to falls in consumer demand because of hard times during the recession. In addition, increased competition has led to increased choice for customers, who at the same time are becoming more sophisticated. Suppliers are dealing with more experienced buyers, who are now more likely than before to know their rights. Expectations of quality and reliability are also rising. The technological revolution has had a major effect on many organisations and occupations, replacing a large number of low-skilled manual jobs, and producing software packages that are now so easy to use that most managers are able to perform some of the traditional tasks previously undertaken by their secretaries. In the face of these pressures, companies have been forced to reduce their costs and the size of their workforce in order to maintain a reasonable level of profit and keep their products and services competitively priced. For some companies, this has actually meant the difference between staying in business or closing down. Others have either merged or been taken over by a bigger organisation.

From a career and job-search viewpoint, understanding what is happening in the world of work is important. Inevitably, this escalating rate of change has had an effect on the character of the labour force and the range of employment opportunities, a situation that will undoubtedly continue to evolve in the future. Let's now examine what is likely to happen to the job market in the next decade.

THE CHANGING JOB MARKET

An overall increase in the labour force is predicted, accompanied by changes in its composition. More women will enter the labour market, accounting for 48% of the working population by the year 2007, while the number of working men will decline slightly. Population growth combined with new entries to the labour market will result in an expansion of the labour force from 29.7 million to over 31 million in 2006. Around three-quarters of this increase will be women occupying part-time jobs.[1]

Occupations in decline will include low-skilled jobs, e.g. factory operatives, farm labourers, unskilled manual workers. However, there has also been a shift away from craft and skilled manual occupations, which were particularly badly affected by the recession, and is indicative of the decline in manufacturing. Continuing job losses are expected in agriculture, engineering and manufacturing. There may also be a reduction in clerical and secretarial jobs largely because of the impact of new technology.[2]

Based on current trends, job growth will largely take place in the service industry. The sectors that are expected to show future growth are financial and business services, distribution, travel, hairdressing and domestic services, hotels and catering, with the largest increase occurring in the public services, particularly education and health.[3]

It is important to understand that the service industry is not simply about providing services to individual customers, e.g. hairdressing, vehicle repairs, supermarket sales and restaurant meals. It is also providing organisations with a whole range of specialised services that they will want to outsource rather than do themselves — building maintenance, computer installation and servicing, office cleaning, transport, catering, legal and accountancy support and some human resource services such as staff

---

[1] *Review of the Economy and Employment: Labour Market Assessment*, Institute of Employment Research, March 1998. *Occupations in the Future: The UK and the Regions, Business Strategies*, March 1998.
[2] Ibid.
[3] *Labour Market and Skill Trends*, DfEE 1998/99.

recruitment. Because of our ageing population, healthcare and social services will be a major provider of jobs.

Professional occupations such as managers, accountants, engineers, doctors, teachers (subjects such as physics, maths, languages and design are in particular short supply) and lawyers are set to grow significantly, as are associated professional occupations such as healthcare occupations including nurses, physiotherapists and radiologists, etc.

Jobs in Information Technology will also continue to grow well into the next decade. The range of organisations employing IT staff is enormous. There are manufacturers of computers and microchips, and electronics companies employing thousands of people in the design and development of computer hardware and software. There is likely to be an increasing demand for software engineers, systems engineers, developers and administrators, Internet developers, project managers, programmers and systems analysts. New jobs will also be created in IT training and consultancy.

Over one million extra jobs will be created in the professional and associated occupations group, mainly driven by the increase in employment in the public services and in financial and business services. More modest increases are expected in sales occupations.[4]

Skill shortages and rising demand for graduates are not only causing employers to develop increasingly sophisticated recruitment techniques, but are also prompting them to look at their ability to retain recruits. The number of companies having difficulties filling their graduate vacancies has increased every year since 1993. However, it would seem that employers would prefer to suffer a recruitment shortfall than take on a graduate without skills such as numeracy and business awareness.

Graduates most in demand will be those who have a degree in the fields of engineering, science and technology, and computer studies.[5] Vacancy trends for graduates suggest a probable increase of between 10% and 18%

---

[4] Ibid.
[5] Ibid.

during the year 2000 over 1999. As a comparison, output of new graduates is rising by 3.5% a year according to the Higher Education Careers Services.[6]

The graduate labour market is no longer typified by a few large organisations with annual intakes well into three figures. They have been joined by many other organisations whose intakes are often smaller. Evidence suggests, however, that job seekers still tend to target the traditional, well-known organisations, while overlooking the newcomers.[7]

These changes in the structure of employment affect the demand for certain skills. The rise in customer expectation and the increasing competition between organisations has led many employers to recruit people with a greater range of skills. The movement towards a more service-orientated economy is contributing towards the current change in skill requirement within occupations. How, then, will the trends that have taken place in the job market affect employers' skill requirements in the future?

'A 1999 survey of 269 senior professionals responsible for recruitment revealed that nearly three-quarters of companies were suffering labour shortages, compared with six in ten during 1998. The most common reason given for difficulties filling vacancies was a lack of experience on the part of applicants, closely followed by a lack of technical skills.

'80% of employers in the public sector reported recruitment problems compared with 68% in the private sector. In both sectors, organisations were most likely to find professional posts hard to fill followed by IT, computing and engineering. The easiest jobs to fill were manual and skilled manual.'

Survey of HR managers by the Institute of Personnel and Development, 1999

WHAT EFFECT IS THIS HAVING ON CAREERS?

The majority of organisations no longer offer a career for life; instead, they present opportunities to develop skills that

---

[6] *Graduate Recruitment and Sponsorship: the 1998 IRS survey of employer practice.*
[7] Ibid.

guarantee your employability. Lifetime careers in one organisation are being replaced by multiple careers in several. Even within the same organisation, an employee can have many roles.

Change and uncertainty are here to stay. New jobs appear and old ones disappear, as some industries recede in importance and others emerge. The likelihood that you'll change your employer much more frequently and have to retrain regularly has made the development of your key transferable skills much more important.

> 'Organisations are becoming flatter and less hierarchical; this means that "lateral promotion" is becoming more common, with staff developing their skills and expertise without necessarily climbing the corporate ladder.'
>
> *Roles for Graduates in the 21st Century –*
> *Association of Graduate Recruiters*

Technology will have a considerable impact on jobs, with employers insisting that their employees use new technology to a far greater extent than in the past. In fact, most employees will require a greater skill level than before, so investing in your own education, training and development will undoubtedly improve your job-search prospects.

Organisations undertaking structural changes, cutting costs and striving to increase efficiency are far more likely to ask their employees to take on extra responsibility. In the past, if an employer couldn't cope with customer demand for better quality and service, the answer would have been to recruit more staff. Organisations can no longer afford to throw money at problems in this way. Instead, they now expect a higher degree of commitment from their staff. In this new world of work, you must accept that flexibility is essential if you wish to succeed. Taking two examples – the sales representative and the secretary – how might this affect their roles in practice?

In the face of commercial pressures and increased competition, companies will expect their sales people to adapt to longer opening hours, undertake a wider range of tasks and display a greater knowledge of their employer's products or services. As well as oral, written, listening and telephone communication skills, employees will have to undertake telesales in those organisations where this is replacing face-to-face selling.

The role of the secretary has changed significantly. Gone are the days of routine typing and working for a single manager. Secretaries are now expected to work for a team of people, and regularly take on some of their manager's responsibility or become IT trainers. With increased export trade, the requirement for competence in foreign languages is also becoming more important.

'Employers can't be responsible for your career, you have to take charge of it yourself. Those who expect companies to do so are often disappointed. Chances are no one will ever care more about your career than you do.'

Managing director – insurance industry

REMEMBER

✓ All organisations are in a continual state of change. To survive and prosper they have to grow.
✓ Changes in the workplace have taken place as employers reacted to falls in consumer demand during the recession.
✓ Most companies have had to reduce costs in order to maintain a reasonable level of profit.
✓ The total labour force is predicted to increase to 31 million by the year 2006. Women will account for 48% of the working population by the year 2007. The number of part-time jobs will also increase.
✓ In the next decade, the number of low-skill jobs will decline and there will be a reduction in clerical and secretarial jobs.
✓ Employment sectors expected to grow are finance, business services, distribution, travel, hairdressing and domestic services, hotel and catering, with the largest increase occurring in public services.
✓ Professional occupations are set to grow significantly with over one million extra jobs created in this group.
✓ Graduates most in demand will be those with a degree in engineering, electronic and electrical engineering, science and technology, and computer studies.
✓ Employers are recruiting people with a greater range of skills.

What are employers looking for?

If you were starting up your own business and needed an assistant, you'd have to answer the following questions:

- What is the nature of the job?
- What type of person would do this job most effectively?
- How can I find someone suitable to fill the job?
- How can I determine which candidate would best fit my requirements?

This chapter will take a closer look at the first two questions.

WHAT IS THE NATURE OF THE JOB?

Job analysis

Much is known about the recruitment and selection practices of medium-sized and large organisations. Many have their own human resources department where staff are trained in the practice of analysing jobs and writing job descriptions. Job analysis is the process of collecting and analysing information about the tasks, responsibilities and the context of jobs. Its objective is to report this information as a written job description, and sometimes a person specification. Job analysis information is frequently used in the process of recruitment and selection because it is particularly effective in matching individuals to jobs.

Here is a job analysis checklist:

- Establish why the job exists.
- Identify the job title and department in which the post is employed.
- Establish the reporting relationship of the job.

- Identify the tasks involved in the job.
- Examine how, when and why tasks are performed.
- Identify the main duties and responsibilities of the job.
- Note the working conditions (physical, social and financial).

The most common methods used to collect the job-related information are:

- Observing current jobholders at work, noting what they do, how they do it and how much time it takes.
- Interviewing current jobholders and their manager. The interviewer usually follows a structured approach using a set of questions prepared in advance.
- Asking current jobholders to complete a questionnaire about the job.
- If the job is new to the organisation, the manager responsible for the post will prepare a list of the duties and responsibilities of the job. The analyst will then interview the manager to make sure that the information collected accurately reflects the new job.

Job description

When the job-related information has been collected and analysed, it can then be presented in the form of a job description. These can vary in length and detail depending on the purpose for which the job description will be used. For recruitment purposes, job descriptions usually provide basic information about the job under the following headings:

- Job title: Title of the job being described.
- Reporting relationship: The job title of the supervisor or manager to whom the jobholder is directly responsible.
- Reporting to jobholder: The job titles of the posts directly reporting to the jobholder.
- Definition of the overall purpose of the job: A concise description of the overall purpose of the job.
- The main accountabilities and tasks or duties: A list of the most frequent duties in order of importance.

Here is an example of a job description suitable for recruitment and selection purposes:

JOB DESCRIPTION

JOB TITLE: Marketing Secretary

REPORTING RELATIONSHIP: Reports to the marketing manager

REPORTING TO THE JOBHOLDER: No subordinate staff

THE OVERALL PURPOSE OF THE JOB:
The jobholder is responsible for providing a confidential secretarial service to the marketing manager and secretarial support to the marketing department.

MAIN ACCOUNTABILITIES AND TASKS:
- Use word-processing and spreadsheet software; prepare correspondence, reports and presentation material.
- Organise meetings between manager and internal/external parties. Maintain diaries.
- Attend all departmental meetings and keep notes for preparing minutes.
- Keep records of staff holidays, sickness and other reasons for absence.
- Receive and sort managerial mail, drawing attention to urgent matters.
- Make travel arrangements and hotel reservations in accordance with the manager's instructions.
- Maintain department library, keeping records of books out on loan. Bring details of new publications to the attention of the manager.
- Maintain records and confidential files so that the manager may have immediate access to essential information.
- Deal with telephone enquiries courteously and efficiently.
- Organise collection and delivery of parcels.
- Ensure stationery levels are adequate at all times.

WHAT TYPE OF PERSON WOULD DO THIS JOB MOST EFFECTIVELY?

Having prepared a job description, the next step is to match the characteristics of the job with those of the candidates. To do this, companies have to decide on the type of person who would do the job most effectively. This description is most commonly known as a person specification.

Person specification

The aim of a person specification, also known as a recruitment or personnel specification, is to outline the qualifications, knowledge, skills, experience and personal strengths required to perform to a satisfactory standard the tasks or duties contained within the job description. A person specification may also have information about special demands, such as the physical conditions of the work, unusual hours or travel away from home. It may also contain terms and conditions of employment, such as salary, benefits, hours and holidays. A candidate's suitability for a particular job is then based on a comparison of his or her knowledge, skills, experience and personal strengths with those outlined in the person specification.

Here is the person specification for the post of marketing secretary shown earlier:

PERSON SPECIFICATION

PHYSICAL MAKE-UP
Essential
In good health and subject to satisfactory company medical report.
Presentable appearance. Clear and well-understood speech.

ATTAINMENTS
Education – Essential
GCSE standard of education with English Language as a pass subject.
City & Guilds or similar standard in typing skills (40 wpm).
Education – Desirable
GCSE grade one English Language.
Job Experience – Essential
Two years' experience of secretarial work.

GENERAL INTELLIGENCE
Essential
Good verbal reasoning ability with logical thought.

SPECIAL APTITUDES
Essential
Good oral and written communication skills.
Good PC keyboard skills.
Capable user of Microsoft Word.

INTERESTS
Essential
Evidence of some non-work related interests.
Desirable
Involvement in social activities.

PERSONALITY
Essential
Able to get on well with people. Self-starter.

CIRCUMSTANCES
Desirable
Current driving licence.

TERMS & CONDITIONS OF EMPLOYMENT
Salary £13,500 pa. Non-contributory pension scheme. Hours of
work 9 am to 5.45 pm.
Monday to Friday. Holidays 20 days pa.

A recent development in the use of person specifications is the inclusion of competencies. Competence in its broadest sense consists of the application of clusters of related knowledge, skills, abilities, personal strengths and motivations by individuals to the successful achievement of a job. To identify those clusters of knowledge and skills, employers study high-performing occupants of the same job. What emerges is a blueprint of the skills and personal strengths that make a difference between outstanding and average performance in a particular job. These findings are then included in the person specification and systematically applied to the assessment of candidates applying for the same job.

Here are three examples of competencies, followed by indicators of behaviour that contribute towards high performance in the job of marketing secretary:

- **Competence:** Concern for quality.
  Indicators: Evidence of minimising errors and maintaining high quality of work by checking.
- **Competence:** Ability to communicate.
  Indicators: Expresses ideas in a clear, straightforward manner.
  Speaks clearly and confidently in person, and on the telephone.
  Listens carefully and responds to verbal and non-verbal messages.
  Evidence of producing well-constructed letters. Uses own initiative to correct grammatical errors.
  Conveys a positive image to others.
- **Competence:** Organising.
  Indicators: Evidence of following up with others to evaluate progress of tasks.
  Identify own tasks to be accomplished.
  Prioritise own tasks.

Most of what you have read so far in this chapter applies to medium-sized and large organisations with human resource departments. Much less is known about the recruitment and selection practices used in small businesses. Although individually such companies recruit small numbers of people, the sector as a whole accounts for the vast majority of job vacancies and turnover.

Small companies are unlikely to have human resources staff, and so the selection task will probably be added to someone's normal duties. Whilst this may imply that small companies will be less likely to use modern recruitment and selection practices, it's clear that more and more are beginning to appreciate the value of job descriptions and person specifications.

REMEMBER

✓ Organisations recruiting staff are faced with two questions:
  • What is the nature of the job?
  • What type of person would do this job most effectively?
✓ Job analysis is the process of collecting and analysing information about tasks, responsibilities and the context of jobs.
✓ The objective of job analysis is to produce a written job description and a person specification.
✓ Job descriptions include the job's main accountabilities and tasks.
✓ Person specifications are used to match the characteristics of the job with the characteristics of the candidates.
✓ The inclusion of competencies in person specifications is a much more recent development. Competence consists of the application of clusters of related knowledge, skills, abilities, personal strengths and motivations by individuals to the successful achievement of a job.
✓ Small companies will be less likely to use modern recruitment and selection practices. However, more are beginning to appreciate the value of job descriptions and person specifications.

3 Self-assessment

Self-assessment is crucial to the process of job search. You must get to know yourself and develop clear career goals that reflect an understanding of what you're looking for in a job and what you have to offer employers. Your career goals may change as you learn more about yourself, but this will only help you focus more clearly on choosing a satisfying and lasting career.

Job search must never be entered into lightly. To be successful, you must be prepared to invest adequate time and think of it as a full-time job in itself. Don't be tempted to rush through the process of self-assessment because you're unemployed or anxious to start sending out copies of your CV. Remember, this is the foundation on which the whole of your job-search structure will rest. Without self-assessment, you will be unable to manage your career or take responsibility for your own future. Even if you're happily employed, this chapter will help you update your inventory of skills and assist your personal development.

MYTH BUSTER

I've been told that all I have to do is send out enough CVs and wait for someone to invite me for interview

Wrong! Waiting for something to happen is bad advice. As a rule, good things don't 'just happen'. Successful people make them happen. Effort usually equals results. As a rule, the harder you work at job search, the sooner it ends.

Self-assessment consists of identifying:

- What you can do ➡ Your experience-based skills.
- Who you are ➡ Your personal qualities or characteristics, personality and temperament.
- Your values ➡ Your attitudes and beliefs.

Establishing answers to these questions will enable you to make sound logical career choices and market yourself effectively. You'll be better informed to make long-term decisions that affect you, your partner and family.

EXPERIENCE-BASED SKILLS

We have all envied those who had ambition and knew from an early age what they wanted to be. Most of us, however, agonised over our future, finding it difficult to be objective about our skills and how these could be translated into careers. This is something we don't necessarily get any better at describing as we grow older. We often fail to recognise skills that don't necessarily correspond with our paper qualifications. For many people this means wasted years travelling in the wrong career direction.

Whether you are at the beginning of your career or considering a career change, think for one moment just how crucial the content of your CV is to your success as a job searcher. If you do not truly understand yourself, this will limit your perception of what you are really good at. The content of your CV must reflect this, and yet your career and your future happiness at work depend on getting this right. Self-assessment is like selling a product: to be successful, a sales representative must know as much as possible about the product and what it can do.

The process of self-assessment therefore underpins any CV and job-search strategy. It enables you to identify your strengths and take a positive view about improving your weaknesses. As a result, you'll be able to give a much more confident account of yourself during interviews and won't be caught out if interviewers ask you to reveal your weaknesses.

'Skill' is often the most misunderstood word in the world of work. It's best described as **the capacity to accomplish successfully something requiring special knowledge, talent or ability, natural or acquired through education, training or experience**. However, it is quite common to mistakenly think of skills as personal qualities or characteristics. For example:

- 'Shows initiative'
- 'Able to take risks'
- 'Is diplomatic and tactful'
- 'Remains calm under pressure'.

Rather than being examples of 'What you can do', these are in fact descriptions of the style adopted by people in the performance of their skills. They are an important part of 'Who you are', which will be fully explained later in this chapter.

Begin the process of identifying your skills by setting aside some quiet uninterrupted time. This will help to clear your head of other unrelated thoughts and allow you to focus on the task at hand. You'll need a pen and several blank sheets of paper.

Think about the following periods of your life:

- **What did you achieve in university, college or school?** Consider exam results, awards, certificates or diplomas attained, your best subjects, commendations from teachers, involvement in extra-curricular activities. Level of school responsibility: e.g. house captain, prefect, etc. Include correspondence courses and evening classes. Did you learn to speak any foreign languages?
- **What have you achieved at home?** Consider how you structured your day and allocated time. How you managed the family budget and organised family holidays. What help have you given to family or friends?
- **What have you achieved at work?** Review all your part-time, full-time and temporary jobs, and the experience you have acquired. Do you belong to any work-related organisations? Have you done any military service?

- **What have you achieved in your leisure time?** What sports do you play and how successful have you been? Have you captained or trained any teams? Have you organised any social events? Have you received any special awards or certificates? Were you a Scout or Guide? Do you have any artistic talent or can you play any musical instrument?
- **What have you accomplished within your community?** Have you undertaken any voluntary or charity work? What have you done for your church or for political organisations?

At this point, you should be listing activities or tasks and not skills. Think of an activity as describing an area of responsibility that requires a set of tasks. Some tasks are related to employment: for example, an accounts clerk checks a set of figures, a secretary organises a meeting and an electrician rewires a house. Others are accomplished in the course of our daily lives: for example, paying the gas bill, preparing a meal and collecting children from school. Tasks are also part of our recreation, hobbies and unpaid work. The purpose of gathering all this information is to produce a melting pot of ideas you can use to identify skills. Think positively and 'blow your own trumpet': undue modesty might mean that you leave out something others would find important. Give yourself the benefit of the doubt and put everything down on paper.

MYTH BUSTER

A degree is a guarantee of a good job

It depends upon the individual's definition of a 'good job' but graduates should remember that in the graduate job market they are competing with other graduates.

Most applicants will have a degree, therefore it's their transferable skills and personal strengths that will sell their application in competition with that of the next graduate.

The next stage is to review your list of activities and tasks to identify your skills. Ask yourself: 'What did I know how to do that helped me accomplish those things?' If you lack the necessary qualifications or feel despondent because you've been out of work for a long time, don't despair. You will need to think carefully about the skills you have acquired in your social or student life. You'll soon find there are all kinds of experience that will be valuable to an employer – you just need to know what they are and how to present them.

IDENTIFYING YOUR TRANSFERABLE SKILLS

Transferable, or 'life', skills are skills that you learn as you move from job to job or that you may have acquired at school, college, university, home or whilst undertaking voluntary, charitable or sporting activities. Carefully evaluate how these skills could transfer to other opportunities. If you are seeking your first job, or returning to employment after a long absence, transferable skills will be particularly important in your job search. When you apply for a job, the employer will want to know what you have to offer. Your answer will be to describe your transferable skills.

Transferable skills can be divided into the following five families:

- people skills
- reasoning and judging skills
- co-ordinating skills
- information skills, and
- originating skills.

Having reviewed your list of activities and tasks, prepare a second list of your transferable skills using the examples in the following exercise as a prompt. Look at each family of skills in turn. Tick the first box against any of the examples if they apply to you and add any others that are appropriate. Consider how well each skill is developed and tick the second box for any that you would like to develop more fully. In the last box rank each skill according to which you consider to be your strongest asset, number one being the most important.

TRANSFERABLE SKILLS

People skills	Tick this box ✓ if this skill applies to you	Tick this box ✓ if this skill needs further development	Rank each of your skills
Advising – Recommending a course of action.			
Caring – Having a strong feeling or concern for others.			
Coaching – Guiding the activities of others.			
Communicating – Conveying, receiving and sharing information.			
Contacting – Keeping in touch.			
Counselling – Helping people with personal, emotional and work problems.			
Delegating – Handing over tasks to subordinates. Briefing them correctly and monitoring their performance.			
Encouraging – Inspiring someone and instilling them with confidence.			
Handling complaints – Dealing with grievances, justified and unjustified, from staff and members of the public.			
Influencing – Persuading someone to alter or agree with a particular course of action.			
Instructing – Teaching. Making known to someone what you require him or her to do.			
Interviewing – Assessing someone's suitability for a job. Obtaining information using a questioning technique.			

People skills cont'd	Tick this box ✓ if this skill applies to you	Tick this box ✓ if this skill needs further development	Rank each of your skills
Leading − Encouraging individuals and teams to give their best to achieve a desired result.			
Listening − Gathering information whilst establishing rapport with the speaker.			
Managing − Deciding what to do and then getting it done through the effective use of resources.			
Mediating − Bringing about a settlement, agreement or compromise between two or more parties. Acting as a liaison between competing interests.			
Negotiating − Setting objectives, deciding on strategy and persuading and bargaining to get agreement and commitment.			
Organising − Getting things done in a well-ordered, efficient and methodical manner.			
Selling − Persuading someone to buy a product or service.			
Speaking in public − Communicating with an audience to motivate, inform or entertain.			
Supervising − Overseeing and inspecting work or workers.			
Training − Bringing a person or group of people to an agreed standard of proficiency by practice and instruction.			

	Tick this box ✓ if this skill applies to you	Tick this box ✓ if this skill needs further development	Rank each of your skills
Reasoning and judging skills			
Analysing – *Examining in detail to break down into components or essential features.*			
Appraising – *Evaluating programmes or services, judging the value of something, evaluating the performance of people.*			
Calculating – *Performing mathematical computations, assessing the risks of an activity.*			
Decision-making – *Choosing between priorities and options.*			
Designing – *Inventing, describing and depicting the parts or details of something according to a plan.*			
Editing – *Checking and improving the accuracy of documents.*			
Evaluating – *Judging or assessing the value of something.*			
Generating alternatives – *Producing a choice between two or more items or courses of action.*			
Innovating – *Creating and developing new ideas or solutions to problems.*			
Interpreting data – *Explaining or clarifying the meaning of facts or figures.*			

Reasoning and judging skills cont'd	Tick this box ✓ if this skill applies to you	Tick this box ✓ if this skill needs further development	Rank each of your skills
Investigating – Analysing, evaluating and seeking new solutions.			
Problem-solving – Using reason to reach solutions.			
Reviewing – Examining to determine whether changes should be made.			
Shaping – Planning and moulding something into a desired form.			
Validating – Assuring the certainty of something in order to dispel any doubt.			

Co-ordinating skills			
Administering – Taking charge of an area of work or tasks.			
Arranging – Making preparations and plans.			
Assembling – Gathering together a collection of parts.			
Constructing – Building parts together as a whole.			

Co-ordinating skills *cont'd*	Tick this box ✓ if this skill applies to you	Tick this box ✓ if this skill needs further development	Rank each of your skills
Controlling – *Comparing what is being achieved with what should have been achieved and, when appropriate, taking corrective action.*			
Co-ordinating – *Blending things together to achieve a desired result.*			
Developing – *Expanding or improving to an enhanced state.*			
Driving – *Operating and guiding a motor vehicle.*			
Erecting – *Raising or constructing (a building, for example).*			
Fitting – *Installing, connecting or attaching.*			
Identifying priorities – *Establishing the best order.*			
Inspecting – *Examining carefully and critically for flaws.*			
Liaising – *Contacting and communicating on a regular basis.*			
Mechanical dexterity – *Able to work with machinery.*			
Monitoring – *Observing and checking.*			
Operating equipment – *Being in charge of a working piece of equipment.*			

Co-ordinating skills *cont'd*	Tick this box ✓ if this skill applies to you	Tick this box ✓ if this skill needs further development	Rank each of your skills
Optimising – *Making the most effective use of something.*			
Planning – *Formulating a programme for the achievement of an objective.*			
Predicting – *Forecasting outcomes.*			
Timing – *Organising time efficiently so that tasks are completed in a set period.*			
Trouble-shooting – *Locating and eliminating sources of trouble.*			

Information skills			
Budgeting – *Outlining the cost of a project; assuring that spend will not exceed available funds; using money efficiently.*			
Classifying – *Arranging or organising according to class or category.*			
Clerical – *Describing skills used by those working in offices.*			
Compiling – *Gathering numerical and statistical data, accumulating facts about a given topic.*			

Information skills cont'd	Tick this box ✓ if this skill applies to you	Tick this box ✓ if this skill needs further development	Rank each of your skills
Computing – Describing skills used by operators of high-tech equipment.			
Corresponding with – Communicating by letter.			
Data-gathering – Collecting information for analysis.			
Diagnosing – Investigating and determining the nature of a problem.			
Dispensing information – Giving out information in various formats.			
Drafting reports – Preparing provisional documents, the content of which are subject to approval before being released.			
Fact-finding – Discovering accurate information.			
Information extraction – Drawing out information.			
Numerical – Working effectively with numbers.			
Observing – Watching carefully.			
Recording – Keeping an account of events or facts to serve as a source of information for the future.			
Researching – Investigating or enquiring in order to gather information about a subject. Physical observations.			

Information skills cont'd	Tick this box ✓ if this skill applies to you	Tick this box ✓ if this skill needs further development	Rank each of your skills
Surveying – Inspecting or examining in a comprehensive and detailed way the condition or quantity of a given subject.			
Updating – Keeping a file of information up to date. Completing records or acquiring new information on an old topic.			
Writing – Communicating using the written word.			

Originating skills			
Achieving – Successfully accomplishing something because of effort, skill or perseverance.			
Anticipating – Staying one step ahead. Being able to sense changes before they happen.			
Creating – Producing new ideas, plans and new ways of looking at things.			
Establishing – Creating and setting up something.			
Initiating – Beginning or introducing something.			
Promoting – Raising awareness in others of a subject's benefits.			

Originating skills *cont'd*	Tick this box ✓ if this skill applies to you	Tick this box ✓ if this skill needs further development	Rank each of your skills
Responsibility-taking – *Willingly taking control of something.*			
Visualising – *Being able to picture things in the mind.*			

Now that you have identified your transferable skills, it is important to understand that employers will ask you to demonstrate, with specific examples, the skills you possess. People often fail to describe their transferable skills adequately. If you can't find such examples in your first list of activities and tasks, spend some time getting this right.

You may also have noticed that each list contains a mixture of skills, ranging from simple to complex. Understanding whether a job requires a simple, complex or a variety of skills will help with your job search. For example, jobs requiring only elementary skills are often closely supervised, whilst jobs requiring more difficult skills are far less supervised and have a greater freedom to act. This information is important for when you come to align your particular strengths with the right job.

By putting in this effort during the early stages of your job-search programme, not only will you have identified your transferable skills but you will also recognise your strongest skills and those that require further attention. This process is a snapshot of your skills at a certain point in time. Even if some of your skills need improvement, your personal qualities will demonstrate to an employer whether you have the motivation and determination to make the improvements.

YOUR PERSONAL STRENGTHS

Understanding who you are is another vital aspect of job search. You may find this part of self-assessment rather difficult because you are not accustomed to confronting reality in this way. However, having a deep understanding of yourself and therefore knowing your personal strengths and weaknesses makes it possible to promote your strengths and minimise your weaknesses.

Success in a job often depends as much on personality as on transferable skills. Recognising and understanding your personal strengths will support the transferable skills you identified earlier in this chapter. So, don't underestimate the importance of your personal strengths: in particular, motivation and a good work attitude are qualities that many employers value. Personal strengths are also particularly important for people who are seeking their first job or returning to employment after a long absence.

To identify your personal strengths, review your first list of activities and tasks and look for evidence of achievements at work, university or college and home. Next, carefully consider the following list, choosing those strengths that you feel have played a role in these achievements. Finally, tick one of the three boxes to rate whether these strengths played a small, moderate or significant part in your achievements.

Personal strengths	Achievement rating		
	Small	Moderate	Significant
Able to maintain confidentiality			
Able to work under stress			
Accurate			
Adaptable			
Ambitious			
Assertive			
Caring			
Confident			

Personal strengths	Achievement rating		
	Small	Moderate	Significant
Conscientious			
Courageous			
Creative			
Decisive			
Dependable			
Diligent			
Diplomatic			
Enthusiastic			
Even-tempered			
Flexible			
Genuine			
Good under pressure			
Helpful			
Honest			
Imaginative			
Independent-minded			
Intuitive			
Inventive			
Loyal			
Organised			
Original			
Outgoing			
Patient			
Perceptive			
Persistent			
Positive			

Personal strengths	Achievement rating		
	Small	Moderate	Significant
Practical			
Punctual			
Quick-thinking			
Rational			
Reliable			
Resilient			
Resourceful			
Responsible			
Self-disciplined			
Self-reliant			
Self-starting			
Shows initiative			
Sociable			
Spontaneous			
Strong work ethic			
Sympathetic			
Tactful			
Tenacious			
Thorough			
Thoughtful			
Tidy			
Tolerant			
Trustworthy			
Truthful			
Understanding			
Versatile			

The danger when carrying out this exercise is that you may be inclined to project your ideal personality. Unconsciously, you may reflect this in your choice of strengths and rating, either because you have not realised your limits or because you don't accept not being able to achieve the career progress you believe is rightly yours. Any discrepancy between the self-image you wish to present and your real personality will hinder progress with your job search. So, be completely honest with yourself, otherwise you'll continue to feel frustrated at your lack of progress. To help you achieve a more objective picture of your personal strengths, involve someone you can trust to tell you the truth, even if this may hurt your feelings.

IMPROVING YOUR WEAKNESSES

No examination of personal strengths would be complete without an honest identification of your weaknesses. This is your opportunity to think about what may hold you back from achieving your career goals. Do you have any personal characteristics, habits or traits you believe may hold you back in your career? Is there any aspect of your character that puts you in an unfavourable light? Do you have any habits that lead to reproaches from your friends and colleagues inside and outside of work?

Opposite are some examples of weaknesses to act as prompts, but it's important to prepare your own list. Take your time. Make sure your list is complete and that you have been honest but not too hard on yourself. Then ask the same person who helped with your personal strengths to provide feedback on your weaknesses.

Whilst identifying your weaknesses is important, it is even more important to understand them. This is best achieved by identifying the situations in which these weaknesses are demonstrated. Only by doing this can you begin to appreciate how they can damage your career objectives and take steps to remedy them. Revealing your weaknesses can be damaging unless you have learned how to transform them into good qualities. In an interview, for example, faced with the question 'What are your

Weaknesses

Avoids confrontation	Meddlesome
Blinkered	Naïve
Dogmatic	Obsessive
Domineering	Obstinate
Emotional	Over-cautious
Forthright	Perfectionist
Impractical	Quarrelsome
Impulsive	Reckless
Inconsiderate	Self-opinionated
Inconsistent	Too demanding of others
Indecisive	Uninspiring
Laid back	Workaholic

weaknesses?' the rule is to present your faults positively, or at least to render them as inoffensive as possible. They should be minor faults that have little influence on your job performance and merit as a potential employee.

Finally, a quick mention of personality tests, since employers, headhunters and recruitment consultants use them in the selection process. Personality tests are designed to assess aspects of personality relevant to work such as interpersonal relationships, work attitudes and values, flexibility and the way people approach work. Any test that provides an insight into your personality can be of enormous value in helping you with your job search. However, if you get the opportunity to take one of these tests outside the field of job search, make sure that you receive feedback. The subject is explained in detail in the third book in this series, *Interviews & Assessments*.

'I've never had what I consider a graduate job, and after nearly two years of routine admin jobs, I began to wonder just where my career was going. A friend of mine arranged for me to take several personality questionnaires and I was given some very helpful feedback. This helped me to understand why I was not settled in my current job. It also left me feeling that I really did have something worth offering to potential employers.

> 'After completing the questionnaires, I drew up a plan to apply for jobs that suited my skills and personal characteristics. I was recently offered and accepted a good job that I really enjoy.'
> *Trainee public relations officer*

YOUR VALUES

Each of us has developed a system of values that allows us to make choices and decisions about what we will and will not do. For example, we decide where we want to live and the sort of house to buy. We make decisions about the type of car to own and where to go on holiday. We make regular decisions about which clothes to wear and what we should do with our leisure time.

Your values are also critically important to any career decisions you make. Consider the length of your working life and the influence your values have on your happiness and that of your dependants. It follows that if you choose to pursue a career that is at odds with what you consider important, you won't be happy with your choice.

Of course, it may not be possible to achieve a perfect match between your values and your career choice, but it remains the key to job satisfaction. If you get stuck in a job in which you have little or no interest, then the job will be hard to do well.

Work-related values, once they are identified, are not capable of precise measurement, nor do they need to be. What *is* important is that you try to determine the presence or absence of these values in the nature of the work you are considering.

Here are some examples of career values. Think carefully about the questions these values raise and what your answers say about you and your career. When you consider career and job options, be sure they support your value system. Although these examples may help, you must generate your own written list of career values.

Values affecting your choice of job

Which of these career values are important to you in terms of job satisfaction? Keep a note of your answers and consider them carefully in the process of choosing a career.

- Contributing to society: *Doing something to contribute to the betterment of the world.*

- Excitement: *Experiencing intense or frequent excitement in the course of work.*

- Financial rewards: *There is a strong likelihood of accumulating large amounts of money or other material gain.*

- Helping others: *Helping other people in a direct way, either individually or in small groups.*

- Influencing others: *In a position to change the attitudes or opinions of other people.*

- Interacting with the public: *Having a lot of day-to-day contact with people.*

- Intellectual challenge: *To be rewarded as a person of high intellectual prowess or acknowledged as an expert in a given field.*

- Job security: *Being assured of keeping my job and a reasonable financial reward.*

- Job stability: *Having a work routine and duties that are largely predictable and unlikely to change over a long period.*

- Making decisions: *Having the power to decide courses of action, policies, etc.*

- Managing: *Being responsible for the work of others and the processing of information or data. Guiding the activities of a team and having responsibility for meeting the objectives of an organisation or department.*

- Opportunities to be creative artistically: *Engaging in creative work in any of several artistic forms.*
- Opportunities to be creative generally: *Creating new concepts that don't follow a format previously developed by others.*
- Peer-group respect: *Respect from those I work with.*
- Physical challenge: *A job that makes physical demands that I would find rewarding.*
- Potential for advancement: *Encouragement is provided for career progression.*
- Power and self-respect: *Controlling the work activities or destinies of other people.*
- Professional status: *Being recognised as a member of a professional organisation.*
- Supervising: *Directly responsible for the work done by others.*
- Time freedom: *Having responsibilities that I can carry out according to my own time schedule.*
- Working as part of a team: *Having a close working relationship with a group or working as a member of a team towards common goals.*
- Working independently: *Able to determine the nature of my work without significant direction from others.*

Your employer

Consider the type of employer best suited to your values. Manufacturer or service provider? Would you be happier working for a small company with fewer than 100 employees or would you prefer to work for a much larger company with 1,000 or more employees? Do you want to work for a young, risk-taking company or one that is more conservative and stable? Do you prefer working in a chaotic atmosphere or an easygoing and congenial atmosphere? All organisations have different cultures.

These determine the work, behaviours and accomplishments that will be rewarded and valued by the particular organisation. You need to evaluate whether the values of the organisation for which you plan to work match your own values.

MYTH BUSTER

Graduates only work for large, blue-chip organisations

Wrong! The DfEE has estimated that 926,000 degree-holders work in the UK for companies with fewer than 250 employees. Although it is true that large companies are retaining their already significant share of the graduate market, more graduates are starting work with small- and medium-sized organisations.

Your finances

It is important to be realistic about how much money you need to live on. Look carefully at your lifestyle and consider your financial commitments. Then compare this with how much you're likely to earn from your chosen career. Will you be paid a guaranteed salary or payment by commission only? Can you expect merit increases and payment for overtime? You may find that salaries in your chosen career are not sufficient to cover your outgoings. If this is the case, you'll need to reconsider and balance your values.

Be prepared to price yourself right in the market, particularly if you're returning to work after a long period of absence or unemployment. Whilst we would all like to be paid a generous salary, ask yourself what you can realistically anticipate and how flexible you could be.

Family considerations

It is essential to take your family and their needs into account. Have you consulted your partner about your choice of job? Will the education of your children be affected? If you or your partner have ageing parents, will your new job permit you the time to keep an eye on them?

Moving house

Much of what has been said about family considerations also applies to location. If you can't move away from where you live at present, then you must accept that this will affect your choice of job. However, if you are prepared to move, this will increase your chances of finding work today. Of course, you must give some thought to where you might want to live and consider all the financial implications. For example, could you afford to increase your monthly mortgage repayments? Consider all the emotional needs of you and your family and be prepared to discuss any move with them.

CAREER CHOICES

Now that you have considered your career values you are ready to summarise your self-assessment. Remember that employers select people who have the skills and personal strengths that best match the job, and that people are happy in their work when their job is consistent with their values. This is why self-assessment is so critical to career planning.

SELF-CONFIDENCE

Throughout our lives, we are influenced by work, family, friends, education and society generally. Unfortunately, some of that influence produces negative thoughts about what we are capable of achieving.

Lack of confidence can hinder our effectiveness when it comes to job search. We all fall into the trap of comparing ourselves with others who may be better qualified or skilled. This is a mistake and can seriously damage your self-confidence. Instead, realise how original and unique you really are and take a positive approach to life. This is the key to gaining self-confidence and, combined with your self-assessment, can bring about job-search and interview success.

To change your self-perception, make the most of the work you've undertaken for self-assessment. This clearly demonstrates that you have transferable skills, personal strengths and values. By focusing on these, and not on your weaknesses, you can accentuate the positive and eliminate the negative.

In the process of job search, you have to face up to rejection and learn to bounce back. Job search can sometimes be a lengthy exercise, so put rejection behind you, and try to get on with life. One way to avoid feeling sorry for yourself is to give every job application your very best attention. Never be tempted to take short cuts; it simply does not pay off. Focus on the career goals you've set yourself and never waver from these. Also, take some time out for yourself, your partner and family. Just because you're job searching doesn't mean you can't still enjoy yourself!

REMEMBER

Self-assessment
✓ Job search must never be entered into lightly. To be successful, you must be prepared to invest adequate time and think of it as a full-time job.
✓ Self-assessment is the key stage to laying the foundation for the whole job-search process.
✓ Self-assessment consists of identifying what you can do, who you are and your values.
✓ You must get to know yourself and develop clear career goals that reflect an understanding of what you're looking for in a job and what you have to offer employers.
✓ Self-assessment will enable you to make sound logical career choices and market yourself effectively.
✓ Because of self-assessment, you will be better informed to make long-term decisions that affect you, your partner and family.

Transferable skills
✓ To be successful in job search, you must identify your transferable skills.
✓ Understanding the nature of your skills is important when you come to align your particular strengths with the right job.
✓ You should also identify the skills that require further development and be prepared to improve them.
✓ For job-searching purposes, employers will ask you to demonstrate, with specific examples, the skills you possess.

✓ Having identified your transferable skills, your CV will more accurately reflect what you can do and you'll be able to give a much more confident account of yourself during interviews.

✓ This is a tool you can't do without and is the best preparation for the subsequent stages of looking for a job and job interviews.

Personal strengths

✓ Knowing your personal strengths and weaknesses makes it possible to present your strengths in the best possible light and to minimise your weaknesses.

✓ Personal strengths are important in career terms, and success in a job often depends as much on personality as it does on experience-based skills.

✓ Employers look for strengths to determine how a person will fit into their organisation.

✓ Weaknesses can damage your career objectives unless you take steps to remedy the situation.

✓ Involve someone you can trust to tell you the truth about your list of strengths and weaknesses.

✓ Personality tests can be useful in assessing aspects of personality relevant to work.

Your values

✓ Our values are the basis on which we make choices and decisions about what we will and will not do with our career.

✓ Values are critically important to your career. If you choose to pursue a career that is at odds with what you consider important, you won't be happy.

Self-confidence

✓ Self-confidence combined with your self-assessment can bring about job-search and interview success.

Conclusion

✓ Summarising your self-assessment serves as a point of reference as you begin your job search.

✓ Employers select people who have the skills and personal strengths that best match the job. This is why self-assessment is so critical to career planning.

✓ Gather as much information as possible about careers. Read the *Insider Career Guides* (see back of book). Cross-match this information with your self-assessment to identify your choice of career and job.

Exploring your options

Once you have a clear understanding of your skills, personal strengths and career goals, you need to prepare a description of the job for which you are best suited. This chapter shows you how to research the job market to identify those employers and jobs that best meet your needs. Here are some points to consider, depending on where you are on the career ladder.

SCHOOL-LEAVERS

For those of you who are leaving school, your interests, ambitions, academic attainments and the job market will almost certainly influence your choice of career. Many young people lean towards a particular field of work because they enjoyed the subject and achieved good grades at school. However, it's not just the subject you have studied but the level of qualification you've achieved that will determine whether you have the entry requirements for a particular field of work. For example, if you've achieved good GCSE grades you could become a trainee computer operator. However, to acquire work as a computer programmer, you'd normally need to have a BTEC Higher Diploma in computer studies or other similar qualification. The state of the job market and the availability of the kinds of jobs you're seeking are also critically important at the start of your career.

UNIVERSITY GRADUATES

It is clear that graduates need more than academic acumen to land the job of their dreams. Today, employers seek a range of skills and personal strengths in addition to a higher education qualification. Such skills might include a logical and analytical approach to problem-solving, creativity, communication and IT. Personal strengths might include working independently and in teams, a 'can do' attitude, a willingness to learn and a commitment to self-development. You may develop some of these skills at university; others you will have to build by yourself. Temporary work, involvement with charities, voluntary organisations or clubs can all improve your job-search prospects.

'26% of graduates would like to work in the media. 25% of graduates said they would like to work in advertising/marketing and computing/IT industries. 75% of graduates have had career-related work experience during vacations.'
The Guardian's *Gradfax Survey*, 1998

'43% of graduates would like to work for a major national or international company; only 19% for a small/medium-sized company.'
Surveyed by High Flyers and published in Graduate Careers, 1998

CAREER CHANGERS

Much is now known about the negative feelings people experience when they are made redundant. However, if you do lose your job it is important to try and get over the initial shock as soon as possible. Use your self-assessment to help maintain a high degree of optimism throughout your job search. Why not use this opportunity to consider changing your career direction, starting a business or updating your job skills by enrolling on a course of further education?

'The impact of redundancy can be devastating ... However, redundancy can bring with it a welcome opportunity to review life and take off in a different direction. For many it provides the excuse to do the very thing they've been putting off for some time.'
Outplacement specialist

Of course, you don't have to experience redundancy to consider a change of career. But whatever your circumstances, always consider your self-assessment and gather as much information as you can about careers that interest you.

RETURNING TO WORK AFTER A BREAK

There are many reasons for leaving work – to raise a family, retrain, even travel the world. Whatever the reason, there may come a time when you wish to return to work. This can be a daunting prospect, and many people worry that their skills might be outdated. Completing a self-assessment will help to identify your skills and a discussion with someone at a local college of further education will establish whether you'd benefit from attending a refresher training course.

Case Study
Returning to work

Joanne worked as a public relations officer in the Northwest office of an automotive product's manufacturer for nine years after graduating. During her career break to have children, she maintained her contacts and did some freelance work for some of these people. She also wrote a regular article about the countryside for the local free paper.

Almost ten years later, she decided to return to full-time work and sent out several speculative applications to employers. One of these offered her a post in their public relations department. Joanne is pleased because she is convinced that maintaining her skills during her career break was the most important factor in making the transition back to full-time work.

RESEARCHING CAREERS AND JOBS

At this point, you will find it helpful to begin preparing a description of the job to which you're best suited. Write down the summary of your skills, personal strengths and values. Then answer the question, 'What are the duties you would like to do in your job?' This list now comprises what you can do, who you are, your values and your preferred job content.

Now you can begin to familiarise yourself with various career fields and what specific jobs entail because this is critical to developing your career goals. School-leavers should visit their local careers service, and graduates should make use of the Graduate Careers Advisory Services. You'll find the

Insider Career Guides published by The Industrial Society particularly helpful in providing information about a range of careers. Another excellent method of gathering information is to talk to people who are working in the same field. As you read about careers, speak with professionals in the field or gain work experience, options that are consistent with your self-assessment will emerge and become the focus of your job search.

SOURCES OF HELP

Larger public libraries are good sources of information about jobs, industries and employers. Together with universities and business school libraries, they often hold extensive collections of reference material. However, it's worth checking out your local library first depending on the nature of your research. Make sure that you are well organised, and establish a system for recording and storing the information you obtain, keeping a note of the sources you've studied, and filing any newspaper cuttings, articles and photocopies.

Often the best way of approaching this type of research is first to take a look at the industry in which you're interested. This should give you an idea of the kinds of jobs that are available. Follow this by researching individual organisations to find out about location, products and services, financial performance, number and type of employees, contact names, addresses and telephone numbers. Finally, move on to examining specific jobs or careers. Current directories that hold information about particular industries include:

- *British Rate and Data* (BRAD). A directory of business publications.
- *Kompass UK.* In seven volumes, this provides an exhaustive guide to 40,000 British companies, identifying them by geographical location, products and services, and describing in tabular form what sort of trading activities they undertake. Published by Reed Information Services Ltd.

- *Macmillan Directory of Business Information Sources.* Gives details of the leading 10,000 unquoted companies registered in Great Britain, including subsidiaries of well-known companies, which are not quoted on the Stock Exchange.
- *Key British Enterprises.* Lists the top 20,000 British companies, detailing the address, when founded, names of directors, type of activity and sales turnover. Published by Dun and Bradstreet.
- *Directory of Trade Associations and Professional Bodies in the UK.* Provides names, addresses, telephone numbers and descriptions of trade associations and professional bodies. Published by Gale Research International.
- *Directory of British Associations.* Published by CBD Research Limited.

Trade magazines

There will almost certainly be a trade magazine covering the industry in which you're interested. These magazines can improve your understanding of the industry and many contain an appointments' section with jobs that may not be advertised in the national press. Here is a small selection of titles:

- *British Dental Journal*
- *Charity Magazine*
- *The Florist Magazine*
- *Hairdressers Journal*
- *The Grocer*
- *Insurance Times*
- *The Stage*
- *Travel Agent.*

Professional magazines

These magazines are published for members of a particular profession. To find out if there are any professional magazines for a particular industry, consult *BRAD* (*British Rate and Data*) – your local library should have a copy. A classified directory of media in the UK, it contains a section of business titles. If your library doesn't have copies of any of the magazines that interest you, they can be ordered from your local newsagent.

Using these sources of information, aim to identify the following:

- Approximately how many organisations are there in the industry and which are the key players?
- Is the industry located in one part of the UK or widespread?
- How successful is the industry? Are their products and services in demand?
- Is the industry developing new products and services?

Now that you have established some helpful background information, refine your research further to identify specific companies that are a good match for you and your values. Obviously the more information you can obtain, the more precise your job search will become. To help with your company research, here is a list of publications that can be found in larger public libraries:

Trade directories

- *The Times 1000.* This is a directory of the top 1,000 largest UK companies, ranked by turnover. Contains data on size, main activity, number of employees and key personnel. Published by Times Books.
- *The Personnel Manager's Yearbook.* Lists prominent companies, with names of personnel and human resource executives and a useful directory of recruitment specialists. Published by A. P. Information Services.
- *Who Owns Whom.* A cross-referencing of interlocking holdings and affiliations. Volume one lists parent companies followed by subsidiaries; Volume two, subsidiaries followed by their parent company. Updated quarterly. Published by Dun and Bradstreet.

- *Confederation of Chambers of Commerce Directory.* Each directory covers the specific part of the country in which you live and lists names of member companies of all sizes, together with contact name, address, telephone number and activity. Some libraries have these in their reference section.
- *Kelly's Business Directory.* Contains information on over 82,000 industrial, commercial and professional organisations in the UK. Provides name, address, telephone number and a brief description. Published by Kelly's Directories.
- *Whitaker's Almanac.* Useful if you need information on employers, societies and institutions, trade associations and unions, industrial research centres, the press, banks, etc. Published by J. Whitaker and Sons Ltd.
- *Handbook of Market Leaders.* Lists who is on top, sector by sector. Published by Extel Financial Ltd.

You should try to build up a picture of the company that includes the following information:

- Full name and address, telephone, fax number and e-mail address of the company's head office. Locations of other company premises.
- The name of any holding company or group.
- The names and titles of directors or senior managers, including the senior human resources post.
- What the company makes, or the services it provides.
- Whether the company is family owned, private or publicly held.
- How long the company has been established.
- Sales turnover and staff numbers.
- Recent company developments, acquisitions and mergers.

Company reports

You may find copies of annual reports for larger companies in your public library. However, these will only be for companies in the particular region. Alternatively, telephone the company in which you have an interest and ask their public relations department to send you a copy.

National, regional and local newspapers

In order to get an accurate picture of how the company operates, its strengths and its weaknesses, it's important to obtain information that has not been produced by the organisation itself. The newspapers available in your public library will provide you with up-to-date information about recent company developments, financial performance, take-overs and mergers.

Careers books

Most libraries have a good selection of careers books and pamphlets produced by industry bodies, including those specifically aimed at university graduates.

Apart from library research, other useful methods of obtaining company information include:

Promotional literature

Most companies produce sales leaflets detailing the products or services they offer. These can provide you with some very useful background information.

The Internet

The Internet is constantly evolving and is an important source of information. Even small companies have websites, and these can provide a good source of information. Profiles of the company usually contain information of special interest to the job searcher, including details of its products or services, names of senior management, and useful addresses and telephone numbers. Larger companies will provide a link to a designated recruitment page with details of current vacancies.

A list of useful search engines with their website addresses can be found in the resource directory at the end of this book. If you don't have the website address for a particular company, try a 'keyword' search on one of these search engines.

National newspapers, including *The Times, Daily Telegraph* and *Observer,* all have websites where you can obtain recent information using a keyword search. These newspapers also provide comprehensive information on CD-ROM on a quarterly subscription. Again, it is worth asking at larger public libraries whether they can provide this service.

Company employees

Another excellent source of information about a company is its employees. Talking to someone who works for the company will give you a good idea about the way it operates and its culture. This is one way of determining whether the company is a good match for your personal values. Contact with company employees may also provide some useful information about the company's recruitment practices and current vacancies.

REMEMBER

✓ School-leavers should bear in mind that it's not just the subjects they have studied but the level of qualification they've achieved that will determine whether they have the entry requirements for a particular field of work.

✓ The state of the job market and the availability of the kind of job you're seeking is critically important at the start of your career.

✓ If you've lost your job because of redundancy, or are considering changing your career for some other reason, use your self-assessment and gather as much information as you can about careers that interest you.

✓ If you're returning to work after a break, and are unsure about the type of work you can do, completing a self-assessment will help you to identify your skills.

✓ Prepare a description of the job to which you're best suited, and write down a summary of your skills, personal strengths and values. Answer the question 'What are the duties you would like to do in your job?'

✓ Familiarising yourself with various career fields and what jobs entail is critical to developing your career goals.

✓ Expand your knowledge about jobs, industries and employers.

Your career summary (CV)

CV stands for Curriculum Vitae, a Latin phrase meaning, for practical purposes, the course of (one's) life. Other synonyms used are 'résumé' and 'career summary'.

A CV is probably one of the most important documents you will ever have to prepare. Without an effective CV, you will never get the interviews you deserve and without them your career will plateau and stagnate. For this reason, you must be prepared to give it the time and effort it warrants.

SELF-MARKETING STRATEGY

The aim of your CV is to get you an interview. To achieve this aim, use your CV as part of a self-marketing strategy applied throughout your job search. Employing the best possible format, use the CV to sell your skills, experience, achievements and potential. An old marketing cliché says 'Give the customer a sample of your product before you expect him to buy from you'. This still works today, gets the customer hooked, and gives him a reason to want more. This principle can just as easily be applied to your CV.

Two important points need to be addressed before you embark on your self-marketing strategy. First, develop an awareness of what you have to offer potential employers. You've already identified what you can do, who you are and your values as part of the self-assessment process. You are now ideally placed to market yourself effectively. Secondly, you must set aside any reservations you may have about self-marketing or promoting your worth and value in the job market. Your CV is your promotional material, so carefully assess the impact it will have on a prospective employer.

> 'The biggest problem with today's CVs is that applicants are far too vague about their skills and strengths. Experience is hardly ever backed up by achievements. Applicants should be using their CV to sell their uniqueness.'
>
> *Recruitment consultant*

BE COMPLETELY HONEST

Although the purpose of a CV is to get you an interview, it's important to remember that the interviewer also frequently uses it to determine the questions you'll be asked during the interview. This is significant for two reasons: First, be completely honest. Don't make inaccurate statements or claims about your experience and skills you cannot substantiate. You can be sure an experienced interviewer will catch you out. Make sure that you can defend everything you include in your CV. Secondly, because you can be certain that some of the questions at your interview will be based on your CV, you can prepare for and practise your replies. As a guide, employers often ask applicants to elaborate further on career goals, education, experience, skills and achievements.

Accepting ownership of your CV is very important. It may well be difficult and time-consuming to complete your own CV, but this is part of the self-learning process that is so important for successful job search. Don't be tempted to pass over the responsibility for completing your CV to one of the many CV preparation services advertised in local newspapers. If someone else composes your CV, the chances are it just will not sound like you.

Once you begin compiling your CV, don't be surprised if your friends and relatives offer you well-meaning advice. Treat all such advice with caution. It can become very confusing and at times a little stressful if you make changes on the advice of one friend only to have this advice contradicted by someone else.

CV FORMATS

The two most familiar CV formats are *functional* and *chronological*. Functional CVs group qualifications and experience into skill areas regardless of when or where those skills were acquired. This format is suitable for those who frequently change jobs or have a long work history in which the responsibilities would be repetitive if listed chronologically. Some employers don't like functional CVs. Their biggest criticism is that they don't show an applicant's career progression within a job, organisation or industry, and information about job titles and the nature of the job are often missing.

Chronological CVs present education and experience sequentially in reverse chronological order. The aim is to give greater attention to the most recent education and experience, and this is appropriate for the majority of new university graduates or for those whose background directly supports their career objectives. This is the style of CV that most employers prefer.

ONE CV OR MANY?

Produce one standard CV and customise this to match the organisation and job you are applying for. Always have a good supply of your standard CV available. If you've given sufficient thought to your transferable skills and personal strengths, this should be satisfactory for most situations. However, a customised CV is the most job-specific and therefore the one most likely to match the employer's requirements.

With a customised CV, you will need to study the employer and their requirements, identify your matching skills and strengths, and then personalise the content of your CV. This is no easy task, but a customised CV can contribute towards a successful interview. Many interviewers will ask you to talk them through your CV. A well-written customised CV can help to direct the interviewer's line of questioning enabling you to 'sell' the skills and personal strengths that best match their requirements. On the other hand, a more general CV may well lead to questions that highlight those parts of your career you would prefer to avoid.

THE CONTENT OF A CHRONOLOGICAL CV
Make a long story short

Most employers prefer short CVs: ideally, no more than two pages. Any longer and they can often deteriorate into a blow-by-blow account of the job searcher's life story. Recruiters find CVs like this boring, and many are sent into sleep mode by lengthy autobiographies. If you're tempted to produce a CV of more than two pages, take a very careful look at the content and ask yourself whether your CV is too wordy.

If you're just starting out on your career as a graduate or school-leaver, then a one-page CV is quite adequate.

Employers and recruitment consultants often receive hundreds of CVs in response to jobs advertised in newspapers and professional magazines. For this reason, it's important to make every word count. The only exception to this rule is where your job is one of those where you are expected to submit a CV with a lot of detail. For example, most senior academics include lists of papers they have had published.

Drafting your CV

Start by entering your **full name** at the top of the page, followed by **your address with postcode** and **telephone number, mobile number** and **e-mail address**. It's no longer necessary to start with the title Curriculum Vitae; this just takes up valuable space.

Age – Enter your date of birth. Do not leave this information out because it will only irritate the recruiter. Many are trained to look for this and will be suspicious enough to reject your CV. If you're concerned that your age may be blocking your job search, try putting your date of birth at the end of your CV.

Personal profile – A personal profile is a word picture of your transferable skills, experience and personal strengths and should take up no more than three short paragraphs. Its use is appropriate for most job searchers except those starting out on the career ladder as a graduate or school-leaver, who would find a career objective more suitable. Examples of career objectives can be found later in this chapter.

Written for maximum impact, the objective of a personal profile is to hook the reader's attention right from the outset. Remember, your CV is selling *you* to the employer. In effect, it is saying, 'These are *my* most important skills and strengths and this is how they can benefit you (the employer)'.

The personal profile should immediately follow your name and address. Employ a bold typeface so that the reader will feel drawn towards the text, and having read the profile will be sufficiently interested to read the rest of the CV.

Use the summary of your transferable skills and personal strengths that you identified in Chapter 3 as the basis for your personal profile. Avoid pomposity or exaggerated descriptions of your skills and strengths. Pick out keywords from your summary and use these to construct two or three attention-grabbing paragraphs. Don't copy phrases from someone else's profile or from the examples in this book. Originality is important to recruiters who regularly evaluate CVs.

Constructing your personal profile will heighten your self-knowledge and boost your self-confidence. The content of your profile can also be used in other job-search opportunities, such as letters of application, telephone conversations with employers and recruitment specialists, and in response to searching interview questions.

Here are some examples of personal profiles to demonstrate the method of construction. This should help you to create your own unique profile.

APPLICANT NO. I

An experienced **MECHANICAL ENGINEER** with extensive experience of production planning in a highly complex environment. Progression has been achieved from craft apprentice to a position on the senior management team, demonstrating ability, and commitment, to the job.

Thorough 'hands-on' knowledge of a wide range of mechanical equipment is combined with effective leadership skills essential to the efficient manufacture of a wide range of engineering components.

Experience also includes repair and renovation of all machinery in the factory complex.

APPLICANT NO. 2

An experienced and qualified **HR OFFICER** with a background in administering and applying personnel policies across a strong unionised workforce. An effective communicator who has provided direction to a small team of support staff by clearly defining the requirements and monitoring output.

A resourceful, positive thinker who is diplomatic, tactful and caring when dealing with people, but whose tenacity and methodical mind produces good organisation and efficient results in problem-solving.

APPLICANT NO. 3

An efficient **MOTOR MECHANIC** with knowledge of a wide range of motor vehicles including **HGVs** and **PSVs**. Able to communicate and relate well to customers; has travelled extensively throughout the **UK** and possesses excellent journey-planning skills.

Sales and service experience includes:
● selling **FMCG**
● handling customer complaints
● maintaining records without constant supervision.

APPLICANT NO. 4

A reliable and conscientious **PERSONAL SECRETARY**. Self-motivated and capable of working on own initiative or as part of a team. Takes pride in completing all tasks to a high standard whilst remaining calm under pressure.

● Possesses excellent keyboard skills.
● Computer literate and fully familiar with most word-processing and spreadsheet software.
● Good communication and organising skills.
● Maintains excellent time-keeping and attendance records.

APPLICANT NO. 5

Creative **ADVERTISING EXECUTIVE** with extensive knowledge of the industry, from both an agency and supplier viewpoint.

Has in-depth experience of analysing situations, drawing conclusions and recommending action plans. Sales ability is well above average with all appraisal objectives exceeded.

Can work well under pressure whilst recognising the importance of completing work on time and within budget. Fluent in French and German.

APPLICANT NO. 6

A **RETAIL MERCHANDISING MANAGER** with considerable experience in the FMCG and retail industry. Successfully influenced customer merchandising decisions whilst making a significant contribution to merchandising development by pioneering the use of a computer system designed to improve space management.

Experience also includes:
- providing sales administrative support on a national basis
- well-proven financial skills.

Possesses strong people management skills together with the ability to negotiate and secure agreements with major companies.

APPLICANT NO. 7

A capable, enthusiastic and self-motivated **TEACHER OF HISTORY** up to and including A level. Recently qualified and now seeking first teaching appointment.

Has a passionate interest in history together with an equally strong desire to teach young people the value of this subject. Excellent teaching, leadership and organising skills combine well with an ability to nurture, motivate and get the very best out of pupils. A positive-thinking person, tactful, caring and sociable who can work equally well as part of a team.

APPLICANT NO. 8

An experienced **SALES PROFESSIONAL**, capable, successful and self-motivated, who works well on his own or as an efficient member of a team. A high achiever with excellent negotiation and customer-contact skills and a successful track record of developing new sales opportunities.

- Resourceful and a positive-thinker who is commercially aware.
- Determination and enthusiasm produce excellent results.
- A sound communicator with an ability to relate at all levels and capable of working to tight deadlines.

Career objective – Graduates and school-leavers can use this as an opportunity to target a particular employer or industry. Set out your qualifications, training, skills and background, and why this makes you suitable for the particular job in which you are interested. Inject some enthusiasm into your objective so that you come across as someone who has thought about his or her career choice. If you're considering more than one type of career, you can create several different career objectives.

Here are two examples of career profiles:

APPLICANT NO. I

A graduate with a 2:1 degree in [discipline]. Self-confident with good communication skills and business awareness gained from work undertaken during vacation and voluntary activities for a local charity. The combination of my qualifications, skills and long-term interest in your organisation demonstrates my enthusiasm and suitability for the post of [job title].

APPLICANT NO. 2

A recent school-leaver with A level passes in [subjects]. Computer literate and capable of high levels of creativity applied to software programmes and Internet web design. Practical experience of the business world was acquired during several placements with IT organisations. My ambition is to join your organisation as a trainee programmer and to demonstrate my strong technical abilities.

Education, qualifications and training – Start with the highest and most recently acquired qualification. For example, if you have a degree put this first and include dates and the name of the institution. Follow this with brief details of secondary education. It's sufficient to put the number of GCE A levels with dates and name of school or college; GCE O levels or GCSEs need not be recorded (see example below). If GCE A levels are your most recent qualification, begin with these, still omitting the GCE O levels or GCSEs.

**1976–1979: Manchester University –
BA in Law (First Class Hons)
1976: Brookfield School: 3 × GCE A levels**

Next, record any special training. If you have attended a lot of training courses, indicate this, followed by several examples of the most relevant ones. At this point, also include any specialist skills and languages you may have.

Membership of professional bodies – Include details of professional memberships, with dates.

Career and achievements – This is the section where you should set out your career progression, beginning with your most recent employer. Include dates, name of organisation, location and job title. Don't leave any gaps. Recruiters are a suspicious lot and may assume the worst. So if you've spent some time travelling the world say so, and demonstrate how it has contributed towards your overall development. Follow this with a **role description**. This should be a brief description (two or three lines) of your chief responsibilities, including the type of business your past and current employers are engaged in and how large they are. Make this interesting and avoid the jargon often found in job descriptions. Recruiters are not interested in seeing a shopping list of your duties. Such a list merely tells the reader what you were expected to do, not what you actually did and, more importantly, how well you performed those duties. Instead of duties, set out your *achievements* to make sure your CV stands out from the rest.

Achievements are tasks that you have accomplished successfully through effort, practice or perseverance using your skills and personal strengths. To compile a list of achievements, look through your employment history, concentrating on what is most recent. Then refer to your list of skills and personal strengths. The work you've undertaken in your self-assessment will now prove invaluable. Think carefully about each job and pick out anything significant or of real interest. Here are some examples:

- You completed an assignment that you did especially well or that you feel proud of.
- You introduced an original idea of your own for your employer. This could be a policy, procedure or perhaps a new piece of equipment.
- Your standard of performance exceeded targets set by your employer.
- You achieved exceptional results in professional examinations whilst sponsored by your employer.
- You demonstrated leadership in the face of challenge.
- You increased sales or profit or reduced costs.
- You opened up new markets for the company's products or services.
- You increased productivity.
- You improved customer care.

Take your time with this part of your CV. Recruiters are strongly influenced by achievements. Don't be modest: this is your opportunity to make your CV stand head and shoulders above the rest.

Employers will be particularly interested in your achievements if you can demonstrate that you have:

- increased sales and profit
- increased new business
- reduced costs
- increased efficiency
- identified and solved problems
- improved systems of management
- improved levels of customer service
- invented a labour-saving or cost-reducing product.

> 'Your achievements are your calling-card for the future. They will help to determine your marketability. In selling yourself, it's results that count.'
>
> *Recruitment consultant*

The best achievements are those that can be shown to benefit an employer. If you're applying for a management position and you can quantify that benefit using numbers, money or volume, so much the better. This is quite a difficult exercise, but well worth the trouble. For non-management jobs, quantifying achievements is unnecessary because prospective employers are mainly interested in your technical experience.

Identifying achievements and how these have benefited the employer is also excellent preparation for the interview. Experienced recruiters are bound to ask you about achievements, but don't be fooled if they use words such as accomplishments, attainments and successes, because they amount to the same thing.

Here are some examples of achievements illustrating quantified benefits to the employer:

- Secured major advances in working practices, harmonising shift patterns and replacing premium-rate payments for overtime with flexitime and time off in lieu. Achieved cost savings of £350k per annum, with no adverse effect on employee relations.

- Increased capacity to meet market demand and achieved record levels of output with a 30% improvement in productivity.
- Successfully streamlined the structure of the factory by merging the production, logistics, engineering and quality functions. This reduced the headcount by 20%, improving communication and increasing efficiency.
- Optimised distribution and transport facilities by liaising with third-party carriers to achieve cost reduction of 20%.
- Increased sales by 127% over a six-year period, positively contributing to an expansion of the company's market share.
- Improved telephone-answering response within customer support to 15 seconds or less, increasing staff morale and customer satisfaction levels.

Notice how all these achievements are written in the immediate past tense. In this way you can avoid using the first-person singular. You can use some business jargon, but always try to tailor this to the reader of your CV.

Skill verbs are important in the construction of achievements. Here is a list of words to help you:

SKILL VERBS

Accelerated	Edited	Maintained
Accomplished	Eliminated	Managed
Achieved	Enabled	Manufactured
Adapted	Enforced	Marketed
Administered	Enhanced	Mastered
Advised	Established	Mediated
Analysed	Estimated	Minimised
Approved	Evaluated	Monitored
Arranged	Examined	Motivated
Assembled	Executed	Navigated
Assisted	Expanded	Negotiated
Attained	Expedited	Observed
Balanced	Extended	Obtained
Built	Facilitated	Operated
Challenged	Finalised	Organised
Channelled	Financed	Originated
Coached	Formed	Participated
Collaborated	Formalised	Perfected
Collected	Formulated	Performed
Commanded	Founded	Persuaded
Commissioned	Gathered	Pinpointed
Communicated	Generated	Pioneered
Compiled	Helped	Planned
Completed	Harmonised	Predicted
Composed	Identified	Prepared
Conceived	Illustrated	Presided
Conducted	Implemented	Processed
Consolidated	Improved	Procured
Constructed	Incorporated	Produced
Controlled	Increased	Programmed
Co-ordinated	Influenced	Progressed
Counselled	Initiated	Promoted
Created	Inspected	Provided
Delivered	Installed	Publicised
Demonstrated	Instigated	Purchased
Designed	Instructed	Realised
Developed	Integrated	Reconciled
Devised	Interviewed	Recruited
Diagnosed	Introduced	Reduced
Directed	Invented	Referred
Distributed	Investigated	Regulated
Diverted	Launched	Reinforced
Doubled	Liaised	Reorganised

Represented	Specialised	Tested
Researched	Stabilised	Traded
Resolved	Streamlined	Trained
Restructured	Strengthened	Transferred
Reviewed	Structured	Transformed
Scheduled	Succeeded	Translated
Secured	Supervised	Tutored
Selected	Supplied	Upgraded
Shaped	Supported	Utilised
Simplified	Taught	Verified
Sold	Tendered	Worked
Solved	Terminated	Wrote

Constructing your achievements is an achievement in itself, but one more word of advice: only include those achievements that are relevant to the job you are applying for. Look carefully at the advertisement, job description or person specification, and match your achievements to the employer's requirements. How many achievements should be included depends to some extent on your career pattern. Obviously, your current or last job is the most important: if you've been in that role for five years or more, then between four and six achievements is sufficient. If you've moved every few years from one employer to another, aim for a maximum of four achievements with each employer.

Leisure interests – There are many conflicting views about this section. Some employers are genuinely concerned about interests, whilst others don't even bother to read them. However, there are certain points to be aware of when deciding what to include. First, be honest and never invent interests. It could be very embarrassing if you were asked to elaborate. Try to establish a balance between your extrovert and introvert interests. Extrovert interests involve social contacts: examples include group sports such as football, chairing the local PTA and membership of a theatre group. Introvert interests usually don't involve other people: examples include gardening, DIY and photography. Listing activities that fall exclusively into either one category or the other is likely to cause concern.

Additional information – Use this space for any other information relevant to your application that cannot be accommodated under the other headings.

CV PRESENTATION

Getting the content of your CV right is vital, but all your effort will be wasted if your CV is badly presented. Aim to produce your own CV using a personal computer and suitable word-processing software such as Microsoft Word or Lotus Wordpro. This way, you will have far greater control of the production and updating of your CV. Alternatively, ask a friend who has a PC to help you out.

Here is a checklist of tips for CV presentation:

- Don't print your CV on coloured paper or present it in a jazzy, colourful jacket. Most employers and recruitment consultants are conservative people who prefer a standard white paper CV. Use good quality white A4 paper, 100 gram or better.
- Choose a standard typeface such as Arial. Don't mix typefaces, and apart from your name at the top of the CV, keep to one font size throughout.
- Don't use flashy graphics; they're not necessary.
- Check your CV for spelling and grammar – ask a friend to check it for you.
- Unless you can produce good photocopies, don't send these as part of your application.
- Don't fold your CV and always send it in a strong A4 envelope, using a first-class stamp. This way, you can be reasonably certain your CV will arrive in good condition.
- Don't send a photograph unless requested. Employers with built-in prejudices may be tempted to discriminate.

Case Study
Curriculum Vitae

Peter, a young electronics engineer, started looking for a new job when it was rumoured that his employer would be making a number of employees redundant. He prepared his CV using his own computer and made use of several of the different fonts in his word-processing package. He was proud of the finished product and each CV was put into a plastic folder before being sent off in response to newspaper advertisements.

After several months, Peter couldn't understand why he was not being selected for interview and decided to give one of the recruiters a call. 'They were very helpful and told me that their advertisement had attracted nearly 100 replies. My CV had been rejected because there was not enough evidence of my experience and skills, and the use of so many different fonts made it difficult to read. I am now concentrating much more on getting the content of the CV right and simplifying the presentation.'

Here is an example of a chronological CV:

DAVID SEARCH MISMM

129 Roman Road • Homefield • Manchester N22 8YD
Telephone 0161 787888 (Home) • 0303 599123 (Mobile)
e-mail dsearch@newline.co.uk

Date of Birth: 22 July 1969   Married with two children

PERSONAL PROFILE
An experienced SALES REPRESENTATIVE, capable, successful
and self-motivated, who works well on his own or as an efficient
member of a team. A high achiever with excellent negotiation and
customer-contact skills and a successful track record of
developing new sales opportunities.

A resourceful and positive person who is commercially aware.
Determination and enthusiasm produce excellent results. A sound
communicator with an ability to relate well at all levels and very capable
of working to tight deadlines.

EDUCATION, QUALIFICATIONS AND TRAINING
Grange High School – Two GCE A levels 1987.
Attended a wide range of sales training courses: e.g. negotiating skills
training, Sundridge Management Centre.
IT training – constructing a database, word processing and
spreadsheets, etc.
Fluent in French.

MEMBERSHIP OF PROFESSIONAL BODIES
Member of the Institute of Sales, Marketing & Management.

CAREER AND ACHIEVEMENTS TO DATE
1994–Present   **SALES REPRESENTATIVE**
                                  Blue Star Animal Foods
                                  Manchester
The Role
Blue Star manufactures and supplies pet foods to veterinary practices
and retail outlets. Current turnover is £20m. Reporting to the Sales
Director, I have responsibility for targeted sales of the company's
products to retailers in the North of England, developing new business
accounts and negotiating discounted contracts with special customers.

Key Achievements
• Consistently achieved all performance standards for sales and
  expansion of the customer base.
• Sales representative of the month four times in the last 12 months.
• Produced and executed a video about Blue Star products for use in
  sales presentations.
• Selected by Blue Star to join a working party creating a new
  sales strategy.

DAVID SEARCH

| 1987–1994 | **BEST FURNITURE COMPANY**
Furniture Manufacturers
Manchester |

| 1991–1994 | **SALES REPRESENTATIVE** |

The Role
Best Furniture Company specialises in manufacturing office furniture. It employs 1,200 staff and has a turnover of £34m. Reporting to the Sales Manager, I was responsible for sales of office furniture to schools and other educational establishments in the Northwest area.

Key Achievements
• Exceeded sales target by an average of 25% per annum during the three years I was in this job.
• Pioneered the introduction of laptop computers for the sales force, improving the quality of customer information available at point of sale.
• Collaborated with the human resources department in the production of sales training courses for induction and negotiating skills.

| 1987–1991 | **SALES ADMINISTRATOR** |

The Role
Reporting to the Sales Manager, I was responsible for providing a comprehensive support service to the sales force.

Key Achievements
• Working with the IT department, successfully created a customer database. This dramatically improved the efficiency of the company's sales and marketing functions.
• Designed a complete set of reporting paperwork for the sales force. This reduced bureaucracy and improved communication with the marketing and accounting functions.
• Negotiated a new motor vehicle insurance policy, providing a better level of cover, breakdown recovery, and saving the company £10k per annum.

LEISURE INTERESTS
Classical music, golf, cricket and swimming.

ADDITIONAL INFORMATION
Current driving licence, free of endorsements.
Willing to relocate anywhere in the UK.

Here is an example of a CV constructed for a university graduate:

PETER HEATH BSc

16 Upton Close • Strawberry Fields • Leeds GG4 2LL
Telephone 01441 525 8989 (Home)
e-mail pheath@newline.co.uk

Date of Birth: 15 October 1976   Single

CAREER PROFILE
A graduate with a 2:1 degree in English Literature. Self-confident, with good communication skills and business awareness gained from work undertaken during vacation and voluntary activities for a local charity. The combination of my qualifications, skills and long-term interest in your organisation demonstrates my enthusiasm and suitability for the post of Personnel Management Trainee.

EDUCATION, QUALIFICATIONS AND TRAINING
East London University – 2:1 degree English Literature 1997
Leeds High School – Three A levels 1994

EMPLOYMENT HISTORY
June–September 1996
Leeds Leisure Centre
Swimming-pool Attendant

Dealing with all visitors to the swimming pool. Ensuring the leisure centre rules were operated correctly and assisting with swimming lessons for school children. I also helped in the leisure centre restaurant, serving meals, dispensing drinks and taking cash.

June–September 1995
Leisure Holidays Ltd, Leeds
Telesales Assistant

Working in the holiday company's telesales department, I was responsible for taking all calls from customers requesting holiday brochures. This necessitated making sure the information was always accurately recorded and presenting an efficient and friendly service to customers.

LEISURE INTERESTS
I play for the local football team whenever possible. Enjoy camping and travelling. DIY car mechanics. Keen volunteer with local charity.

ADDITIONAL INFORMATION
Chair of university debating society.
Active member of senior five-aside football team.
Current clean driving licence.

MYTH BUSTER

The best way to produce a CV is to use one of the software programs designed for this purpose

Wrong! People buy these CV software programs believing they'll make the process a lot easier. Unfortunately, these programs are about filling in the blanks and therefore lack flexibility. The documents they produce all look alike and they're easy to spot when screening CVs. If you personalise your CV it will be far superior to any produced using a software program.

THE ELECTRONICALLY SCANNABLE CV

Some large employers and search and selection consultants now use computers to read CVs. When your CV arrives it will first be scanned into a computer as an image, using optical character recognition (OCR) software. This software examines the image, identifies each letter and number, and creates a text file (ASCII) that the computer can understand. Following this process, the CV is stored in a database.

Whether CVs have been sent in response to an advertisement or kept in a database for future reference, the recruiter will input a series of keywords or phrases based on the job description and person specification. A typical search might include mandatory keyword requirements such as age, qualifications, experience, skills, job titles and level of responsibility, followed by several preferred requirements. The computer system then scans all its records for these keywords and can, for example, recognise skills and qualifications regardless of how well they're written, because it's programmed to use synonyms and acronyms.

Whilst the number of recruiters using computers to scan CVs is currently relatively small, the number is on the increase. Recruiters find this type of system particularly useful when processing large numbers of applications at the first screening stage.

What then are the implications for the job searcher? First, try to establish if the recruiter uses scanning software. If they do, construct a second CV that employs a different approach to the content and format. A copy of the job description or person specification will help you to identify likely keywords. Alternatively, familiarise yourself with the keywords for your job and industry. You should be able to find examples of these in career literature and job advertisements. If you're planning to include a personal profile at the beginning of your CV, the inclusion of keywords is very important. Avoid repeating these same keywords in the rest of your CV by using synonyms instead. This is one way to improve your chances of the computer recognising the words you have chosen to include.

Here's a further checklist to help you get the format right:

- Use a standard sans serif font such as Arial or Helvetica throughout your CV. Apart from your name, which can be 14 points, use sizes between 10 and 12 for the rest of the text.
- Don't use italics, underlining, bold or fancy graphics, because this confuses the scanning software.
- Don't place boxes around text, because this prevents the software from reading it.
- Don't put text on both sides of the paper, because only one side can be scanned.
- Always spell out the words 'per cent' and 'and'. The '%' and '&' signs cause problems for scanning software.
- Put dates *before* any details about education and employers, because this improves the computer's ability to read the dates correctly.
- Aim for plenty of white space on your CV, particularly between sections. This makes it easier to scan.
- Only use paperclips, not staples.
- Don't fold your CV.

REMEMBER

✓ The aim of your CV is to get you an interview. Use the CV to sell yourself, your skills, experience, achievements and potential in the best possible format. Be prepared to give it the time and effort it deserves.

✓ Important points for your CV include developing an awareness of what you have to offer potential employers and deciding on the content and presentation style.

✓ Don't make inaccurate statements or claims about your experience and skills that you cannot substantiate.

✓ When compiling your CV, treat all advice you receive from friends and relatives with caution.

✓ The two most familiar CV formats are functional and chronological. Employers prefer chronological CVs.

✓ Produce one standard CV content and, whenever time permits, customise this to match the organisation and the job for which you are applying.

✓ Almost 90% of employers surveyed prefer between one and three pages for the ideal CV.

✓ Consider including a personal profile in your CV. This is a word picture of your transferable skills, experience and personal strengths, and should be no more than three short paragraphs long. Graduates and school-leavers should consider including a career objective.

✓ Setting out your achievements in your CV will make it stand out from the rest.

✓ If you know that your CV will be scanned, consider constructing a second CV using a different approach to the content and format.

THE PRINCIPLES OF GOOD TIME MANAGEMENT

Job searching is a job in itself. If you're currently employed, then balancing work for your current employer and conducting an effective job search is not going to be easy. If you're currently unemployed, then this will still require planning and you must assign it as much priority as you would any task undertaken for your previous employer.

The principles of good time management are essential for job search. Simply jotting down interview arrangements in you pocket diary and turning up on time isn't good enough. You need to plan and organise your job search, set priorities and stick to deadlines. Failure to do so will almost certainly result in loss of control and stress. Make sure you continue all the other aspects of your life, so you can see how critical it is to create time for the important things.

To organise yourself, you need a disciplined approach to the management of time. If you have a laptop computer or scheduling software for your desktop computer, then make good use of them. But really all you need is a good diary and a simple method of keeping track of your applications. What is important is setting priorities and sticking to them. If you're currently out of work, this brings a real sense of urgency to your job search. Time really is at a premium.

WHAT YOU NEED TO MAKE A START

Space and equipment

Begin by setting aside some space of your own. This could be a spare bedroom or a table set up in your dining room. Access to a telephone is vital, and consider buying or borrowing an answerphone, because there is nothing worse than losing opportunities because no one was there to answer the telephone. Alternatively, subscribe to BT's Callminder service. This enables you to retrieve your messages using the digital keypad on your telephone. A computer and printer are not essential for job search, but they do make life a lot easier. If a PC is not available, ask friends if they can help or consider paying someone to do this work for you. Whilst faxing copies of your CV is not to be recommended, some recruitment consultants may ask you to do this if there's a degree of urgency. If you don't have a fax machine, many high-street printers or stationers provide a faxing service. Always send the consultant a further copy of your CV by post. This ensures that they have a decent copy to show their client.

> 'Always make sure your telephone will be answered, even if this means using an answering machine. If a potential employer is unable to reach you, you could end up losing a valuable job opportunity.'
>
> *Recruitment consultant*

Stationery

You will need a good supply of the following stationery:

Paper
Always use white A4 paper of good quality (100 gram or more). Good presentation is so important, and there are many different brands available from your high-street stationer. It's best to buy paper by the ream (500 sheets), since you'll need this sort of quantity for a professional job search. It's also more economical to buy in bulk. Use this paper for your CV, covering letters and other correspondence. Make copies of all your correspondence on a cheaper paper (white A4, 80 gram).

Envelopes
Always use A4 envelopes, preferably white, alternatively manila. When sending out speculative applications to employers, write the words 'private and confidential' underlined, immediately above the name of the recipient. Although this doesn't guarantee that the addressee will open your application, without it, a junior clerk in the post-opening department may get to see it first.

For letters without CVs, use white envelopes, but not the window type.

Postage stamps
Always have a good supply of first-class stamps to send off applications.

A4 notepad
Use a notepad to record details of telephone calls and to itemise 'things to do'.

Ring-binder files
These make an ideal home for your filing system. Using guide cards for the different sections will make them easier to access.

Clear plastic wallets
These are good for keeping copies of advertisements and newspaper articles together.

Paperclips and stapling machine
Use paperclips when sending out your CV and covering letter. The stapling machine is useful for keeping your file copies together.

AN OFFICE ROUTINE

When you're in your office routine, peace and quiet are essential. This can be quite difficult in households with young children, but you must come to an arrangement with your partner that frees you from the frustration this sort of disruption would cause.

YOUR FILING SYSTEM

Setting up an effective filing system is important for keeping track of all your applications. Divide them up so that it's easy to distinguish between responses to advertising (visible job market) and speculative applications (the hidden job market). Keep your applications in date order and give each a reference number. For control purposes, you need a simple form to show the current state of play with each application. Here's an example:

APPLICATION CONTROL DOCUMENT

Date of application	Company name	Source of vacancy	Job title	Date reply received	Follow-up date (if appropriate)	Interview date	Outcome of application

Source of vacancy = Newspaper title, recruitment consultant, employment agency, jobcentre, speculative application, etc.

PROGRAMMING YOUR ACTION

Effective management of time means planning your action for the week ahead. If you do this, you will soon learn to prioritise your job-search activities. Here's a sample routine you can adapt to suit your own circumstances:

SAMPLE ACTION PLAN FOR JOB SEARCH

	Morning	Afternoon	Evening
Monday	Open incoming mail. Check newspapers for job advertisements. Prepare CVs and letters of application in response to advertisements. Review routine for the rest of the week.	Prepare speculative applications. Make telephone calls to recruitment consultants.	Spend one hour in research at public library. FREE TIME
Tuesday	Open incoming mail. Check newspapers for job advertisements. Prepare CVs and letters of application in response to advertisements. 11.30am – visit J Smith recruitment consultant.	Plan interview strategy for Thursday's interview with Jones Engineering. Check route and journey time.	Begin preparing list of contacts for networking. FREE TIME
Wednesday	Open incoming mail. Check newspapers for job advertisements. Prepare CVs and letters of application in response to advertisements. Prepare speculative applications.	Spend one hour in research at public library. Practise answering interview questions in preparation for Thursday's interview, and prepare a list of your own questions to ask the employer.	Telephone Bill Davis, contact from previous employer. FREE TIME (early night)
Thursday	Rise early. 8.15am – set off for interview. 11.15am – interview with Jones Engineering.	Review interview performance from morning. Keep notes. Open incoming mail. Check newspapers for job advertisements. Prepare CVs and letters of application in response to advertisements.	Continue preparing list of contacts for networking purposes. FREE TIME
Friday	Use Internet to access online recruitment companies. Make speculative applications.	Open incoming mail, etc. Make telephone calls to contacts from last week's social meeting.	Discuss contact list with my wife. Read and check daily papers for job advertisements.
Sat/Sunday	Sunday – check papers for job advertisements.	FREE TIME	FREE TIME

Case Study
Organising yourself

Graham, a 40 year-old office manager in the building industry, was made redundant. He was positive enough about searching for his next job and set about organising his daily routine. After a few weeks, Graham and his wife began to argue over everyday matters. He was used to leaving for work early in the morning, whilst his wife, who was a secretary, left much later after having breakfast and reading the morning newspaper. The problems began when Graham moved his PC onto the kitchen table and started preparing letters and CVs early in the morning. To make matters worse, after a full day of job searching, Graham would collapse in front of the TV and fall asleep. When his wife returned home from work, it seemed to her that Graham had been asleep for most of the day.

Graham said, 'We talked this problem through and this helped us to understand each other's viewpoint. Setting priorities and putting time to one side for our social life helped enormously.'

THE INTERNET – A WORD OF CAUTION

The role of the Internet in job search is dealt with in detail in the next chapter. However, a word of caution is appropriate when deciding how best to manage your time for job-search purposes. There are plenty of job sources open to the serious job searcher, so make use of as many of these as possible and don't rely on the Internet too heavily. It can be rather hypnotic and before you realise it, the whole day will have passed by. Remember, the Internet is no substitute for human contact.

REFERENCES

You must decide who will provide references to support your application. Names of referees should not appear on CVs, but many organisations ask for this information on their application forms. When you're offered a job, it will usually be subject to the receipt of satisfactory references. This means they can withdraw the offer should any reference prove unsatisfactory. For this reason, act now and take care in choosing your referees. Contact each referee, apart from your current employer, and make sure that they're happy to supply a reference that will meet your requirements. Consider providing a referee for each employer on your CV, as well as two character references from people outside of work.

It's not a good idea to take references with you to an interview. Employers hardly ever accept them, preferring to write to your referees requesting a reply to specific questions in their letter or questionnaire.

REMEMBER

✓ The principles of good time management are essential for job search.

✓ Plan and organise your job search, set priorities and stick to deadlines.

✓ You need a good diary and a simple method of keeping track of your applications. Setting priorities and sticking to them is important.

✓ To start with, you need office space, office equipment and stationery.

✓ Create an office routine.

✓ Setting up an effective filing system is important for keeping track of all your applications.

✓ Effective management of time means planning your action for the week ahead. Use a form to organise this.

The visible job market represents all vacancies that are advertised in the public domain. Most advertised vacancies appear in newspapers, magazines, journals and the trade press. However, there are several other areas in which job advertisements can now be found including the Internet, jobcentres and the Graduate Careers Advisory Services.

MYTH BUSTER

Most vacancies are advertised in newspapers and magazines

Wrong! It is estimated that only 15% of the available vacancies are advertised in newspapers and magazines. The cost of newspaper advertising has risen so much that employers have found it necessary to find alternative, cost-effective means of recruiting staff such as the Internet. However, job searchers should understand that newspaper advertising is still an important source of job vacancies; it's a matter of apportioning the right amount of time to each of the sources presenting the greatest opportunities.

SOURCES OF ADVERTISED VACANCIES

Newspaper advertising

The volume of spending by employers on this form of advertising has fallen considerably and the growing trend is downwards. It's estimated that only 20% of vacancies are available through the visible job market: of these, 15% are advertised in the press and the remaining 5% are filled using the Internet and other sources. Another fact seems to be that employers are modifying their advertisements in an attempt to improve their recruitment process by discouraging unsuitable applicants, and by ensuring that they have a better idea of the demands of the job.

National daily newspapers and weekend newspapers are an important source of vacancies for the job searcher. Several specialise in advertising jobs for particular sectors, whilst others carry jobs across all areas. Some national papers also publish a regional edition, attractive for organisations that are particularly interested in recruiting staff from the North or the South. A list of national newspapers with details of the sectors they cover, and on which days of the week, can be found in the resource directory at the end of this book.

Many companies prefer to advertise in regional and local newspapers. These are published on a daily, evening or weekly basis, either paid for or free. Try to get hold of as many of these as you can, according to the requirements of your search.

Trade and professional magazines

Many trade and professional magazines carry job advertisements. If you're professionally qualified, then you will receive your magazine as part of your membership benefits. Alternatively, check with your public library to see if they have copies. A list of trade and professional magazine titles can be found in the resource directory at the end of this book.

HOW TO RESPOND TO ADVERTISED VACANCIES

Sending CVs

If you're responding to an advertised vacancy, you can guarantee that your CV and covering letter will end up in a pile with hundreds of others. From these, the employer will select five or six people for interview. When an employer receives so many replies, the screening process can be ruthless, with 75% or more applications weeded out before they're passed to the recruiting manager. As part of this process, a young member of the company's human resources department will probably scan your letter and CV. In the recruitment world, this is known as the 'thirty-second scan'. This person may have little in-depth knowledge of the advertised position, but will have been given a person specification to use as a checklist against which your application will be measured. If you don't measure up to the person specification, then no one else will ever see your letter and CV.

Minimising the risk of rejection is therefore very important. This means getting the content and presentation right and differentiating yourself from the mass of applications.

When you've found an advertisement that interests you, study it carefully to identify the employer's exact requirements. Look for words that describe responsibilities, experience, skills and other qualities. Does the advertisement tell you anything about the company? What is the salary? Where is the job based? Write all of this information down and try to establish the order of importance for the employer's requirements.

When you're satisfied with the information you've gathered from the advertisement, check whether it matches your own skills and personal strengths. If it does, then you may wish to consider personalising the content of your CV.

Your covering letter

The covering letter is another opportunity for self-marketing. Never think of it merely as wrapping paper for your CV, or send a CV without a covering letter. The covering letter is your opportunity to go beyond the CV, to customise it to suit the employer and their requirements. This means you should avoid sending covering letters with a generic content. Many job searchers squander the covering letter opportunity, when it is a chance to give the recruiter a real sense of your transferable skills and personal strengths. After all, what's the point of producing a really good CV if you send it with a letter stating '*I am enclosing a copy of my CV for the post of Sales Representative recently advertised and hope to hear from you soon*'?

Customising your covering letters means thinking carefully about the employer's requirements and raising the employer's awareness of your skills and strengths that go beyond the basic requirements. Think of your letter as a business proposal, not as a plea for an interview. Try to focus on their needs and how you can satisfy them.

Your letter should be businesslike but conversational. Avoid using stiff formal language such as '*Enclosed please find my CV for your perusal*' or '*I look forward to receiving your acknowledgement of this application in due course*'. Get to the point right from the start. For example, '*Please accept this application for the post of Computer Programmer advertised in the* Daily Telegraph *on Thursday 25 May 2000.*'

Next, look again at the information obtained from the advertisement and, using bullet points, set out in the letter the key elements of your background, experience and achievements that match the recruiter's requirements.

Make sure you comply with any instructions in the advertisement: for example, quoting reference numbers or providing salary details. Aim for the best possible presentation using good quality paper, preferably the same used for your CV, and keep to the same font size. Finally, check the letter for correct spelling, grammar and punctuation.

'A covering letter should not restate the information contained in the CV. This is not very interesting from the recruiter's viewpoint. Make a point of telling the recruiter how you match up to their job requirements.'

Human resources manager – motor industry

Here is a typical newspaper advertisement:

SENIOR SALES REPRESENTATIVES

£25k pa plus commission　　　　　　　　**North & South**

We are a well-established company manufacturing personal computers. With a planned expansion programme that includes a restructuring of our sales function, we plan to recruit two new senior sales reps based in the North and South of the country.

You will be responsible for the sale of our products to specific corporate customers who demand exceptional service and quality. You will also be required to expand our customer base and assist in the induction training of newly appointed sales staff.

We require a minimum of four years' experience in a similar role with computer literacy, plus personal qualities of determination, perseverance and a willingness for self-development.

Salary and benefits are above average for the industry. Fully expensed company car. Assistance with relocation will be provided.

Send your CV with covering letter, quoting reference HSA9, details of current salary and why you should be selected for interview to:

David Smith, Recruitment & Development Manager
Fab Computers Limited
The Trading Estate
Industry Lane
Liverpool PP2 7DD
Telephone: 0151 707 9393

Here is an example of a covering letter replying to this advertisement (for the accompanying CV, see page 69):

Tel: 0161 787 888

129 Roman Road
Homefield
Manchester
N22 8YD
14 August 2000

Mr David Smith
Recruitment and Development Manager
Fab Computers Limited
The Trading Estate
Industry Lane
Liverpool PP2 7DD

Dear Mr Smith

Reference Number: HSA9 – Senior Sales Representative

Please accept this application for the post of Sales Representative advertised in the *Daily Telegraph* on Thursday 10 August 2000.
As you will see from the attached CV, I can offer the following relevant background and experience:

- 9 years' sales representative experience.
- Frequently exceeded sales targets for existing and new business.
- Company sales representative of the month four times this year.
- My strong negotiating skills enabled contracts to be acquired at prices beneficial to my company.
- Particularly skilful at making sales presentations and training new sales staff.
- Computer literate, and completely familiar with a wide range of software.

My current salary details are £23,000 per annum basic salary plus an average of £3,000 commission during the last 12 months.

I am confident that you will find my details are a good match for the skill and experience requirements outlined in your advertisement, and would be pleased to expand on this at a future interview.

Yours sincerely

David Search

David Search

'I particularly like the style of covering letter where the company's requirements appear on the left-hand side of the page and applicants place their matching experience and skills against these on the right-hand side of the page. Because they stand out from the rest, this enables me to see immediately if we have an applicant suitable for interview.'

Technical recruitment consultant

Here's an alternative style of covering letter that enables the recruiter quickly to compare your skills and personal strengths with the company's requirements. For this reason, this style of letter is particularly popular with recruitment consultants and many human resource managers.

Tel: 0161 787 888

129 Roman Road
Homefield
Manchester
N22 8YD
14 August 2000

Mr David Smith
Recruitment and Development Manager
Fab Computers Limited
The Trading Estate
Industry Lane
Liverpool PP2 7DD

Dear Mr Smith

<u>Reference Number: HSA9 – Senior Sales Representative</u>

I am very interested in your vacancy advertised in the *Daily Telegraph* on 10 August 2000. As you will see from the attached CV, I can offer the following relevant background and experience:

<u>Your requirements</u>	<u>My experience and skills</u>
Minimum of four years' experience in a similar role.	• Nine years' experience in a high-pressure sales environment.
	• Frequently exceeded sales targets for existing and new business.
Expand the customer base.	• Proven ability to acquire new customers.

	• Strong negotiating skills highly valued by current employer.
Assist with induction training.	• Particularly skilful at making sales presentations and training new sales staff.
Computer literate	• Computer literate and completely familiar with a wide range of software.

My current salary details are £23,000 per annum basic salary plus an average of £3,000 commission during the last 12 months.

I am confident that you will find my details are a good match for the skill and experience requirements outlined in your advertisement, and would be pleased to expand on this at a future interview.

Yours sincerely

David Search

David Search

If you're a university graduate responding to a job advertisement on your university notice board, here is an example of a letter to send with your CV (see sample CV on page 71):

Tel: 01441 525 8989

16 Upton Close
Strawberry Fields
Leeds GG4 2LL

23 October 2000

Miss G Brown
Personnel Manager
Smith Computers
Sheep Lane
Manchester XY4 2WW

Dear Miss Brown

Reference Number: SC109 – Personnel Management Trainees

Please accept this application for the post of Personnel Management Trainee advertised on our university notice board.

My interest in personnel management began during my vacation employment with Leisure Holidays Limited. I had several helpful discussions with their Personnel Manager and concluded I would be ideally suited to this work. Subsequent research and interviews with careers advisers have confirmed this for me.

My academic and work experience has shown that I can analyse and evaluate problems, communicate and negotiate effectively with a wide range of people, make decisions, meet deadlines and use organisational administrative skills.

Throughout my course, there was a strong emphasis on teamwork and I have undertaken many collaborative projects with fellow students. This has helped me to understand the dynamics of teamwork, vital in any business environment.

My ambition would be to train for the IPD qualification while working as a Personnel Management Trainee. I believe I have many of the qualities you require and would be pleased to expand on this at a future interview.

Yours sincerely

Peter Heath

Peter Heath

Please remember, these are only examples. Don't follow the style in this book slavishly; instead, aim to give your own letters a personal quality.

'Never begin your letter with "Dear Sir" or "Dear Madam". As far as the employer is concerned, if you can't be bothered to spend the time finding out the name of the person you're writing to, then you're not a suitable person for interview. Also, even if the advertisement you're responding to gives the contact's Christian name, don't be tempted to use it. This over-familiarisation will not help your application.'

Career management consultant

COMPLETING APPLICATION FORMS

Apart from sending CVs in response to advertisements, you may be asked to complete an application form. Application forms make it easier for employers to screen applicant information presented in a way that's uniform to all applications they receive. This is used to determine who is suitable for interview, which applicants should be rejected and as an aid in directing the interview. As with CVs, your application form may be screened by someone from the company's human resources department and not by the recruiting manager.

Unlike CVs, application forms enable the employer to decide just how much is revealed about the applicant. Consequently, from your viewpoint as a job searcher, application forms only cramp your style, allowing little room for individuality. However, it's important that you observe all the instructions in these forms if you want your application to make any progress.

Here is a checklist to observe when completing application forms:

- Take your time and make sure you'll not be disturbed.
- Photocopy the form so that you can check the contents before completing the original.
- Read the instructions carefully and observe them.
- Write your application form rather than type it. Trying to type accurately in the small boxes often found on these forms is almost impossible.

- Make sure your handwriting is as neat as possible.
- If you are sent a job description and person specification with the application form, use these to compare with your skills, personal strengths and values.
- Answer all the questions. If a question doesn't apply to you, then write 'Not applicable' in the space provided.
- Take particular care with your response to open-ended questions. Draft and redraft your answers until you're completely satisfied that they're the best you can produce. Make use of your CV and all the information you have collected during your self-assessment.
- Take time to research the recruiting company and try to find a way of including some of your findings on the form.
- Choose each word carefully and avoid exceeding the space provided.
- Make sure there are no unexplained gaps in your employment record.
- Adopt a positive approach throughout the form, leaving out anything negative.
- In some circumstances, it may be helpful to include a copy of your CV. However, never write 'See CV' in answer to questions on the application form; this is bound to annoy the recruiter.
- If the application form asks for referees, make sure you have their permission before including their details on the form.
- When you are satisfied with the draft, transfer the information to the original.
- Keep a copy for reference purposes. This could prove helpful if you're invited for interview.
- Include a brief covering letter, stating which position you're applying for and where you saw the advertisement.
- Use an envelope large enough to return the form, covering letter (and CV if appropriate) without having to fold them. Post using a first-class stamp.

BIODATA

Biodata is short for 'biographical data'. As a selection technique, it's reviewed in more detail in the third book in this series, *Interviews & Assessments*. However, it's included in this chapter because employers use completed CVs and application forms to extract biodata for screening purposes.

Biodata is used by some of the larger employers in the UK, particularly those recruiting graduates. It aims to take the uncertainty and subjectivity out of decisions that rely on that most basic selection tool: the application form or CV. To do this, employers look for similarities in the good performers' experience, demographic background, qualifications, motivation, interests and biographical-type data that distinguishes them from the same job's poorer performers. They obtain this information from their employee's personnel records or from specially constructed questionnaires. Each piece of information is given a mathematical weight to produce a 'score' for each individual. Personal history factors that are found to give the best prediction of future job success receive the most weight in the scoring process.

Application forms used for biodata have usually been designed for this purpose. The information provided on the form then becomes the basis for compiling a biodata score that assesses how vital aspects of an applicant's life history, experience, etc. match the statistically relevant items. A minimum score is often set and the higher an applicant's personal score is above this level, the greater their chances of selection for interview.

Some organisations prefer to use a computerised biographical information blank (BIB). This form asks for much more detailed information and includes questions such as most liked/disliked subjects at school. These specially designed questionnaires usually consist of several pages of multiple-choice questions, with each alternative weighted separately.

If you're sent an application form from a company using biodata as a means of selection, it's highly unlikely that you will be made aware of this. However, if you're sent a BIB, be honest and consistent with your answers. Remember that at an interview, you'll be asked to illustrate your answers. Here is an example of a BIB used to screen university graduates:

BIOGRAPHICAL INFORMATION BLANK

1. Did you obtain any of the following? (Mark as many as apply)
   Entrance scholarship   ( ) a
   Senior scholarship   ( ) b
   University prize   ( ) c
   Travel scholarship   ( ) d
   None of these   ( ) e

2. If you've already graduated, what was the class of your degree?
   First   ( ) a
   Upper second (or individual second)   ( ) b
   Lower second   ( ) c
   Third   ( ) d
   Unclassified   ( ) e
   Not yet graduated   ( ) f

3. Are you studying for a higher degree?
   Yes. PhD   ( ) a
   Yes. Masters degree   ( ) b
   No   ( ) c

4. Typically, how do you arrange your study time?
   To a regular schedule   ( ) a
   In a rush at the last moment   ( ) b
   Whenever you feel in the mood   ( ) c

5. Which of these best describes your attitude to study?
   Serious and thorough   ( ) a
   Moderately concerned   ( ) b
   Generally carefree   ( ) c

6. How do you cope with deadlines for set work?
   By completing it well in advance   ( ) a
   By setting a schedule   ( ) b
   By preparing answers to expected topics   ( ) c
   By crash revision at the last minute   ( ) d
   Make no special arrangement   ( ) e

7. How do you prepare for examinations?

By a scheduled revision programme	( )	a
By preparing answers to expected topics	( )	b
By crash revision at the last minute	( )	c
Make no special arrangement	( )	d

8. Which kind of teaching have you found most congenial?

Supervised research	( )	a
Lectures	( )	b
Essays on set topics (or other set work)	( )	c
Seminars or discussions	( )	d
Personal tuition	( )	e
None of these	( )	f

9. How satisfied are you with the course you have followed?

Completely satisfied	( )	a
Satisfied	( )	b
A little dissatisfied	( )	c
Very dissatisfied	( )	d

10. How well prepared do you usually feel before examinations?

Pretty strong all round	( )	a
Adequate in most areas	( )	b
A bit patchy with some gaps	( )	c
Rather vulnerable	( )	d

11. When you're aware that you have controversial or unpopular views on some topics within your class or group, which is your normal response?

I try to persuade the rest to share my point of view	( )	a
I ignore the others and stand my ground	( )	b
I try to avoid arguments because it leads to bad feelings	( )	c
I tend to go along with the majority	( )	d
None of these	( )	e

12. How much do you contribute to seminars or formal discussions?

Usually the most	( )	a
More than average	( )	b
About average	( )	c
A little less than most	( )	d
Not very much	( )	e

13. Which of these best describes your approach to university life?

Happy-go-lucky	( )	a
Lively and sociable	( )	b
Realistic, putting the qualification first	( )	c
Seriously scholarly	( )	d

14. How do you intend to use your degree?

In further research	( )	a
To get a job	( )	b
As an entry qualification to a career	( )	c
No particular use	( )	d

15. Which of these best describes your involvement in clubs or societies at university?

Held elected positions (e.g. chairman, secretary) in several	( )	a
Held elected positions in one	( )	b
Ordinary member only	( )	c
Not active	( )	d

16. Which of these have you joined in actively at university?

Debating or politics	( )	a
Students union administration	( )	b
Students magazines/newspapers	( )	c
Sport	( )	d
Music, drama, reviews	( )	e
Rag activities	( )	f
Clubs and societies	( )	g
Religious activities	( )	h
Fund-raising for charities	( )	i

17. Mark the leisure activity in which you spend most of your time.

Going out socially	( )	a
Clubs or societies	( )	b
Sport	( )	c
Concerts, theatre, arts	( )	d
Reading	( )	e
Church/charity work	( )	f
Listening to recorded music	( )	g
Radio/television	( )	h
Collecting	( )	i
Model-making	( )	j
Music-making/performing arts	( )	k
Politics	( )	l

Climbing ( ) m
Car maintenance, other DIY ( ) n
Other (please specify) ( ) o

18. Which of these best describes your interest in sport?
Competition ( ) a
For fun and exercise ( ) b
Spectator only ( ) c
Little interest in sport ( ) d

19. How often have you taken vacation jobs?
Never ( ) a
Once or twice ( ) b
Three times or more ( ) c

20. How often do you go out with a group of friends (socially or to places of interest)?
Most evenings ( ) a
Once or twice a week ( ) b
Once or twice a month ( ) c
Seldom ( ) d

21. How important to you are these as sources of news/ current affairs?

	A little	Some	A lot
Radio/television	( ) a	( ) b	( ) c
Daily newspaper	( ) d	( ) e	( ) f
Sunday newspapers	( ) g	( ) h	( ) i
News magazines	( ) j	( ) k	( ) l
(e.g. *Economist*)			

THE INTERNET

The Internet is one of communication's biggest success stories, but many people are still not aware of what it is and how to use it to their advantage. Put simply, the Internet is a vast network of computers that enables the office or home desktop computer to communicate with others.

The Internet was established in 1969 as a means of sending files between computers. Global e-mail has now become the preferred document transfer method for those who have discovered it, as it has solved many of the problems associated with transferring documents between one party and another. Any file can now be sent, including documents, pictures, presentations and spreadsheets, as an e-mail attachment. The reader can download their e-mail, import the attachment into their preferred word-processing or spreadsheet package, change it, and even send it back to the originator. This has particular appeal for recruiters, because they can ask applicants to e-mail their CVs.

In 1992, the technology became available to create the World Wide Web (WWW). This is a vast collection of pages of information, each able to carry text, images, animation and sound. The most significant element of the WWW is the ability of each page to carry a link or 'hyperlink' to any number of other pages on the Web. Each page of information has its own unique address or URL (Uniform Resource Locator). The addresses that appear frequently in newspaper and TV advertising are for an organisation's 'home' page on its website. The WWW offers an exciting opportunity for companies to display their products, services and even their complete catalogues on the Web, employing graphics and sound as well as text. It is possible to re-create an entire company brochure on the WWW and receive opinions from the viewer directly from fill-in forms attached to part of the site.

'For the first time, UK graduate recruiters have rated the Internet as a more popular hiring tool than either the milk round or careers fairs. Recent statistics reveal that almost half of major UK employers now use the Internet for recruitment purposes — a threefold increase on the number of firms with an online recruitment presence in 1997.'

Incomes Data Services, 1999

With an estimated audience of 60 million people worldwide, and this number is rising rapidly, the Internet is a very serious place to do business. Businesses and individuals are joining the Internet at the rate of 4,000 per week.

If you have a PC at work or at home, you may already have access to the Internet and be using it to send e-mails. With the aid of a browser, you can also access the WWW. If you're considering access to the Internet, here are the basic requirements:

Personal computer
You should aim for a PC with 32Mb of RAM, a 166Mhz Pentium processor and at least 2Gb of hard-disk space.

Printer
There is a variety of printers available to suit everyone's pocket.

Modem
You will need this to send data over the telephone network. Most new PCs come with a modem fitted internally. If you have to acquire a modem separately, these can be bought for around £100.

Telephone line
You will have to decide whether you can manage using your existing telephone line or whether a separate line would be more appropriate. Much depends on the volume of calls you expect to make and receive.

Internet access
There are two kinds of Internet access available. Internet Service Providers are organisations that sell their ability to give you Internet access directly, along with support services. Online Service Providers create their own communities that include information such as news channels, sport, book sales and entertainment, as well as access to the Internet.

Browser software
To access the WWW you'll need browser software such as Microsoft Internet Explorer or Netscape Navigator.

Website addresses
The components of a website address can tell you a lot about the site. Here are some examples:

- .net – An Internet service business or one that exists solely on the Internet.
- .co.uk – A commercial company operating in the UK.
- .com – Mainly commercial companies operating in the US.

- .org – A non-profit making organisation.
- .ac – An academic institution.

Search engines
A search engine is a web host that contains millions of web pages. Equipped with a text box into which the search terms can be typed, they will produce a list of websites containing relevant information. From this list, you can select the most appropriate sites for your search. Details of the best of these search engines can be found in the resource directory at the end of this book.

> 'Using the Internet should take the pressure off students, who can relax having filled in just one application form, safe in the knowledge that their particulars are being circulated around hundreds of companies.'
>
> *Manager – online graduate recruitment agency*

Getting connected

If you have a PC with a modem and are thinking of connecting to the Internet, buy one of the Internet magazines such as *Internet* and *Internet Today*. These will provide you with plenty of information on getting connected and the best search engines.

Internet recruitment

Recruitment on the Internet is becoming increasingly popular with employers, search and recruitment consultants, and applicants. Tens of thousands of jobs are advertised weekly on the Internet, with job sites being amongst the most visited in the world. Clearly, you'll need to know how to handle the Internet if you're to make the most of your job search.

From a job searcher's viewpoint, how does recruitment on the Internet work? To begin with, you need to produce your CV using the advice given in Chapter 5 about electronically scannable CVs. You can then e-mail your CV to one or more of the online recruitment agencies, together with information on where you want to work and what salary you're expecting. Here are some examples of online recruitment sites (more can be found in the resource directory at the back of this book):

- The Careers Service Unit (CSU), useful for recent graduates.
  Contact on www.prospects.csu.man.ac.uk
- Workweb offers details of all types of vacancies.
  Contact on www.workweb.co.uk/

'The Internet will change the nature of recruitment advertising. Companies will focus much more on promoting themselves as employers through their website and selling themselves to potential recruits. However, newspaper advertising is so strong in the UK that the Internet is unlikely to kill it off.'
Manager – human resource consultancy

'I like the net. It's a place where you can come obligation-free in your own time, to find out about us. You don't have to dress up smart or say the right thing.'
Graduate recruitment manager – computer manufacturer

All these Internet sites have a facility that allows you to search for appropriate vacancies. However, their usual practice is to carry out a keyword search of their database and then e-mail details of appropriate jobs to the candidate to browse through. From then on, the CV is matched with new jobs every time the database is updated. This service is completely free of charge to the job searcher.

Don't be tempted to register with every online recruitment agency you can find. This will only lead to masses of information coming to you via e-mail, most of which won't be suitable. It's best to browse these sites and find those that specialise in your particular field and job type.

It's clear than online recruitment agencies are speeding up the time it takes to send in your details and link up with prospective employers. Using the Internet, you can easily access job opportunities in most sectors around the world, read detailed information about companies you might want to join, and specify where you want to be based.

> 'I went to a number of recruitment agencies and all said the same thing, "We'll keep you on file". I felt the online recruitment agency was a bit more proactive, and because the form is so thorough, I came up with jobs I would never have considered before. As a result, I'm pretty optimistic about my chances.'
>
> *University graduate*

In addition to recruitment company job sites, it's well worth visiting the sites of specific organisations that interest you. Many large organisations now have well-established websites that include details of current vacancies. Put together your own list of potential employers and browse to see if they publish job vacancies. Apart from vacancy details, you will often find details of company news that could be helpful in your job search.

Case Study
Online recruitment

Recruitment Manager, Recruitment Consultants

'What first attracted us to this online job site was the fact that it covered a range of sectors. It was very important to us that we found a site covering all the industries for which we recruit. With this job site, we rapidly find quality candidates from its vast database. Apart from the online job advertising, we also make use of its e-mail adverts and banner spaces, and these have also proved very effective. On average, we now spend about 50% of our company advertising budget recruiting staff through the Internet.'

Human Resources Manager, Computer Software Manufacturer

'An important part of my job is to recruit experienced IT professionals. Whilst advertising in computer magazines has been useful, it's expensive and our advertisement is one of many. With the online job site we get noticed very quickly and this has proved to be a distinct advantage to us. We're getting an excellent response and are now finding up to 45% of our new recruits through the Internet.'

> **Software Systems Designer**
> 'I recently decided to search the Internet for jobs and within a few days, with the help of the online CV form, I'd applied for several jobs. I was invited for interview for two of these and within a week had accepted an offer of a really good job with excellent prospects.
> 'I was astonished at how quickly the service operated, and unlike normal recruitment processes, which can often be both long and drawn out, my details went to the right people immediately.'

JOBCENTRES

Jobcentres aim to provide a service to all people looking for work. Although their vacancy boards carry vacancies of all types, few senior jobs are handled by jobcentres. It's well worth visiting them regularly, however, as their vacancy boards are often updated. Jobcentre staff can arrange interviews for suitable applicants and offer support and advice.

If you're unemployed and registered with the jobcentre, they will draw up a back-to-work plan for you and inform you about other services that are available, including job-search seminars and job-review workshops. If you've been unemployed for six months or longer, you may be eligible to join your nearest Executive JobClub. These clubs provide advice and support, plus free use of telephone, typewriters, photocopiers, stationery, postage stamps, newspapers and journals.

CAREERS CENTRES

Careers centres help people up to the age of 21 to find work. They have vacancies for young people that jobcentres don't normally advertise. They also advise young people about training vacancies, such as Modern Apprenticeships, many of which may not be advertised in local and regional newspapers.

EMPLOYMENT AND RECRUITMENT AGENCIES

Quite a lot of employers regularly use their local employment agency to find staff. In the past, most vacancies registered with employment agencies were temporary, but the situation has changed and people registered with an employment agency fill many full-time jobs. It's also not unusual for temporary staff to find full-time work through employment agencies, with employers treating the temporary contract as a probationary period.

TV AND RADIO

This form of advertising has declined in popularity with employers. However, some of those who still have plenty of money in their advertising budgets do advertise vacancies through Teletext and on local radio.

THE MILK ROUND

The annual milk round of universities is a recruitment exercise that targets final-year undergraduates. Each year major employers tour the universities searching for the best people who'll graduate that academic year. Their quest begins in October and November with company presentations and careers fairs. Here, you can often collect application forms and copies of graduate recruitment brochures. These tell you more about the companies and their career opportunities. Alternatively, brochures can also be obtained from the careers advisory service in universities and colleges. The process continues with interviews at universities, and ends with second-round interviews at assessment centres. Keep your eye on the university notice boards, as employers use these to advertise their jobs and forthcoming presentations.

All students should visit their university careers advisory service. Whilst they're often very busy places, they're excellent sources of information about employers and many provide a regular weekly vacancy bulletin. If you need advice, it's best to make an appointment.

PROFESSIONAL ASSOCIATION NEWSLETTERS

Many professional associations regularly communicate with their members using monthly newsletters, some of which carry job advertisements. If you're a member of a professional institute, it's worth including this source in your job search.

EMPLOYER'S PREMISES

Some employers still have vacancy boards fronting their premises. Large supermarkets and DIY chains use this approach because their vacancies are seen by thousands of customers.

REMEMBER

✓ The visible job market represents all vacancies that are advertised in the public domain.

✓ Only 20% of vacancies are available through the visible job market; the rest are filled using the hidden job market.

✓ National daily, weekend, regional and local newspapers are an important source of vacancies. Many trade and professional magazines also carry job advertisements.

✓ The key when responding to job advertisements in the press is to minimise the risk of rejection. Get the content and presentation right of both your CV and covering letters.

✓ The covering letter is an opportunity for self-marketing. Always customise your covering letter. Never send a CV on its own in response to an advertisement.

✓ Employers use application forms so that they can easily screen applicant information. Check advertisements to see whether there's a match with your own skills and personal strengths. If there is a match, then consider personalising the content of your CV.

✓ Biodata is a selection technique where employers examine your application form for similarities to those of a good performer in that job. Scoring higher than the good performer improves your chances of selection for interview.

✓ Tens of thousands of jobs are advertised weekly on the Internet. Browse the Internet to identify suitable job vacancies.

✓ Make full use of all other sources of advertised vacancies.

The hidden job market

WHERE ARE ALL THE VACANCIES?

If only 20% of job vacancies are available through the visible job market, where are the rest of the jobs? The answer is that they can all be found in the hidden job market. The term 'hidden job market' refers to vacancies that haven't been advertised, and therefore, generally speaking, aren't in the public domain. These jobs are not so much hidden as simply unseen by those job searchers who view the job market as only advertised vacancies. The hidden job market is therefore a vital part of your self-marketing strategy.

Accessing the hidden job market is about creating your own opportunities. It's a much more proactive method than simply responding to advertised vacancies – although, as explained in the previous chapter, you shouldn't neglect that element of your job search.

The chances of getting a job from the hidden job market are considerably better than from the visible job market. Whilst large numbers of job searchers only respond to advertised vacancies, ensuring that the competition will be fierce, far fewer target the hidden job market, which means that it is less competitive, and potentially far more rewarding.

The hidden job market comprises:

- jobs that are available through headhunters
- jobs that are available from recruitment or selection consultants
- jobs that are available from employment or recruitment agencies
- jobs placed with interim management specialists
- jobs found or created as a result of networking

- jobs found through speculative approaches to employers
- jobs found through outplacement specialists.

In this chapter, we take a close look at how best to approach this rich source of job vacancies.

HEADHUNTERS

Headhunters (sometimes known as search consultants) are in the business of executive search. These jobs are not advertised, because the recruiting organisation has already decided there are very few people in the marketplace able to fill the post in question. Sometimes, the vacancy is of such a sensitive nature that it would be detrimental to the organisation to broadcast the fact that it was looking for a replacement. The organisation may even know the names of likely candidates but needs a go-between to sound them out. The role of the headhunter is therefore to 'search' the marketplace and approach candidates who are considered suitable for the job.

You may be wondering how headhunters can be useful to your job-search strategy. In a job market that is much more open than it used to be, headhunters recognise that there are many very good unemployed people available. If you're looking for a senior post, then you should approach headhunters who deal with your industry and job. Ask your local library if they can obtain a copy of the *CEPEC Recruitment Guide* or *The Executive Grapevine*. Both these publications contain lists of headhunters, including details of their particular specialisation. Some large companies do both search and advertised recruitment and you can identify them in these same publications.

Headhunters keep computerised files on potential candidates, and often these are the first place they look when conducting a search. It's best not to send out your CV to every headhunter; instead, you're more likely to have your CV details entered on a database if you're selective. Begin by checking which headhunters deal with your industry, job type, salary level and preferred work location.

Send each of these a copy of your CV and a covering letter. Be sure to include something in your letter to 'hook' the reader's attention, such as special achievements. Also, include details of your salary and benefit expectation and any other requirements, such as your family's ability to relocate.

Since hundreds of CVs flood into the typical headhunter's office, you may not receive a call acknowledging receipt of your CV. Don't call to ensure your CV arrived: such badgering is unwelcome. However, keep in touch if you change jobs or move to a different address.

Here is a sample of a covering letter suitable for sending with your CV to a headhunter:

Tel: 020 7111 444

28 Manor Lane
Chiswick
London W2L 7BB

27 April 2000

Mr David French
DRD Search Consultants
106–109 Church Road
London W3L 6GG

Dear Mr French

I have ten years' experience in the field of human resources and was appointed to the post of Human Resources Manager with a pharmaceutical manufacturer in 1994. I have decided to seek new opportunities, and have included a copy of my CV on the chance that you may be working on an assignment that could use an HR professional.

My strongest skills include business planning, developing reward and remuneration policies, resourcing and employee development. I would welcome hearing from you.

Yours sincerely

Alan Farmer

Alan Farmer

RECRUITMENT CONSULTANTS

Unlike headhunters, recruitment consultants specialise in advertising all vacancies on behalf of their clients. After taking a brief from their client, they'll prepare a job description and person specification and use these documents to draft the advertisement. They handle all the responses to the advertisement and select a preliminary list of candidates for interview or combined selection test and interview. Following the first-round interview, the consultant selects a shortlist of candidates to be interviewed by the client.

Recruitment consultants vary in their approach to using candidate databases. Some feel that a database is unnecessary because they always advertise the job for their client, and therefore ensure that the information they give to their client is up to date. From the consultant's viewpoint, the drawback of a database is that applicants often fail to inform them about any changes in circumstances. However, many recruitment consultants do maintain a database and these are the ones you should target for your job search. Check first whether they would welcome a CV on a speculative basis. The *CEPEC Recruitment Guide* indicates whether speculative applications are accepted, and also includes contact names. Your covering letter should be similar to the one suggested for headhunters. However, replace the last line with the following: 'I would welcome the opportunity of a short meeting, say twenty minutes, to bring you up-to-scratch on my skills and personal strengths. I will give your office a call in a week's time to arrange this.'

> 'Whilst we welcome speculative CVs from applicants, we also require some specific information on every applicant, and ask that they also complete one of our standard forms. Information from this form is then input into our database. Regrettably, applicants often fail to keep us up to date with changes in their circumstances.'
>
> *Head of recruitment consultancy*

EMPLOYMENT AND RECRUITMENT AGENCIES

Employment agencies are referred to in Chapter 7 'The visible job market', as they often advertise jobs on behalf of their clients. However, they also encourage applicants to register their career details so that they can be contacted when a suitable vacancy arises.

Employment agencies differ from recruitment consultants in that they usually work within a local geographical area, but may be linked by computer to branches in other areas. They also handle a much larger spread of jobs, from entry level up to middle management. Staff in employment agencies may have some training in selection, but often have little knowledge of the industry their clients come from.

Look in your local *Yellow Pages* or *Thomson Directory* for details of employment agencies. It is best to telephone them first to make sure they recruit the job you're looking for, and only select those agencies that have a reasonable number of clients capable of generating suitable vacancies. Ideally, give the agency a copy of your CV as part of an exploratory interview, and only as a last resort send them a copy by post. A meeting with a member of the agency staff is important, because you can use the opportunity to self-market. They're far more likely to try and place you with one of their clients if they can provide first-hand information about you.

Finally, it's wise to keep in touch with employment agencies – usually every three weeks is frequent enough – to check if there have been any new vacancies.

INTERIM MANAGEMENT SPECIALISTS

Interim management, sometimes known as executive leasing, is used by companies who have decided that it would be commercially damaging to leave a management or specialist post empty during the four or five months it may take to recruit a permanent replacement. An unexpected large order, a period of rapid expansion or relocation – all require managing. In all three cases an interim manager would plug the gap and provide the ideal solution.

Interim management is not always short term, however. Some companies require part-time specialist help for long periods. For example, a small company might benefit from the skills of a personnel or public relations manager, but recognise that it would be impractical and far too costly to create full-time posts. By leasing two interim managers for one or two days a week, the company acquires the skills of highly qualified specialists without incurring the prohibitive costs of employing someone permanently.

If you are interested in interim management, details of several companies can be found in the resource directory at the back of this book; alternatively, look in your local *Yellow Pages* directory. Telephone the company first and make an appointment. Be sure to take a copy of your CV with you and tell the company about your skills, personal strengths and achievements.

NETWORKING

Networking is about meeting people formally or informally, on a one-to-one basis or in groups, and making the most of your contacts. As part of the hidden job market, networking is critical in achieving job-search success.

In many companies, any discussions about job creation are usually conducted by a small group of people well before a decision is taken to advertise the job. What you must do is tap into this small group of people and present your CV before the decision to recruit externally is taken. This is what networking is all about.

Begin the process by drawing up a list of people you have had previous contact with, either in a business capacity or socially. Here are some examples:

- business colleagues
- previous employers
- accountants
- Rotary Club members
- Chamber of Commerce members
- former customers or clients
- bank manager
- insurance agent
- solicitor
- relatives
- friends
- doctor
- sports club members
- charity groups.

Deciding who to approach is a matter of good judgement. They must be people who can offer real help with your career. Adopt an informal approach to friends and relatives, since you don't want to damage your relationship. The aim of the first round of meetings is to get your contacts to provide you with more contacts. Your meeting with this second layer of contacts should provide you with yet more contacts. Continue the process until you're put in touch with someone who is party to the process of job creation.

Never ask your contacts directly for a job. This will only cause embarrassment and might lead to your network drying up altogether. Instead, ask for career advice and the names of those who can help with your career plan.

Networking is not for the faint-hearted. It requires skill, diplomacy, self-esteem and assertive behaviour. For more information about building a network, reaching targeted individuals, raising your profile for job-search purposes and career success with sample letters and checklists, see the second book in this series entitled *Career Networking*.

SPECULATIVE APPROACHES TO EMPLOYERS

Apart from networking, it is also possible to make successful speculative approaches to employers, by again tapping into the small group of people who know about vacancies before they're recruited externally.

Don't be tempted to send out hundreds of letters, all with a similar content. This is inviting rejection on the same scale. Instead, set out to identify employers who match you and your values. Refer back to the sources of help outlined in Chapter 4 and make full use of the information available in your public library. Having decided on a particular industry, use the trade directories to compile a list of suitable employers. Rank these employers in terms of personal preference and keep notes of all the information you find. Next, read newspapers, company reports and access the Internet to build up more information about each of these employers.

Employers receive a great many unsolicited job applications. Most of these will fall into the mailshot category.

Their blandness easily identified, their authors will, if they're lucky, receive a polite 'no thank you' letter. To ensure that your application isn't treated in the same way, be prepared to spend time creating personal letters that demonstrate an interest in the company, as well as a well-presented summary of your skills and personal strengths.

Newspapers and the Internet are by far the best way of focusing your search for something current and worthwhile about your targeted company. Information that might prove useful could include:

- relocating to a new site
- opening a new factory or offices
- winning a large contract
- industry awards
- planned expansion programme
- development of new products
- contribution to the local community.

The purpose of your research is to include a summary of the information you've unearthed, and where you found it, in the opening paragraph of your letter. This should grab the attention of the reader, and set it apart from all the others. To keep the reader's attention, you then need to find a way of connecting this to your skills and personal strengths. This should demonstrate that your interest in the company is genuine and that you've done your homework.

It is important to address your letter to the right person. Human resource managers are responsible for recruitment, but they may not always be included in the small group of people who have prior knowledge of any forthcoming vacancies. Therefore, address your letter to the director responsible for the section of the business in which you're interested. Don't assume that the name you have found during your research is the correct one. This person may well have been promoted to another job or even left the company, so telephone them first to check this out.

Here is a sample speculative letter demonstrating these points:

Tel: 0121 313 6666

18 High Street
Sutton Coldfield
Warwickshire
B99 2QZ

15 July 2000

Mr Paul Wilkins
Production Director
Sleepwell Bed Company Ltd
44 Green Park
Birmingham B77 9TJ

Dear Mr Wilkins

I noted in yesterday's *Financial Times* that your company has had an excellent year with record profits, and that you are planning to open a new factory with offices in Sutton Coldfield sometime next year. This was of particular interest to me, because of my long-term ambition to work for your company. Do you intend to recruit a production manager for your new factory?

With extensive experience of production, my achievements include a successful period streamlining the production set-up for my present employer. In addition, my strong management skills and business awareness have proved essential in meeting all my annual key targets. Enclosed is a copy of my CV with additional information about my skills, personal strengths and achievements.

I would be delighted to meet you to explain my interest in your company and why I would make a valuable addition to your management team. I will give you a call next week to arrange a mutually convenient time to meet.

Your sincerely

Simon Brown

Simon Brown

As with all other job-search correspondence, presentation must be to a high standard, with no grammatical or typing mistakes.

Diary a date to call the company and ask for the addressee. If he or she is not in when you call, don't ask them to return your call. They probably won't. Instead, try to find out when would be a good time to call again. Leave a message with their secretary to say that you called and that you'll call again on a particular date.

Case Study
Speculative applications

John recently started looking for a new job. He thought it would be a good idea to send out a lot of letters to companies in the same business as his current employer. He was very disappointed with the result, because only half of the people he wrote to bothered to reply.

Someone suggested he should choose five companies and find out as much as possible about them, then incorporate some of this information in his letters. He received a reply from all five companies and one of them invited him for an interview. John said, 'They were very pleased with my background and experience and have offered me a supervisory job in their telesales department.'

OUTPLACEMENT SPECIALISTS

Outplacement helps people to review their skills and clarify their career objectives. These specialists work for companies who often offer outplacement to employees who have lost their job because of redundancy. Their code of practice prevents these companies from working for individual clients, but many employ freelance specialists who will be prepared to do so. However, there is no reason why you shouldn't conduct your own job search. This book, along with the others in this series, provides you with all the support and advice you could need. On the other hand, if your employer has offered you outplacement as part of your redundancy package, be sure to take it!

As well as providing career counselling services, outplacement specialists have strong links with headhunters and recruitment consultants, so they often hear about vacancies. Present your CV and covering letter in the same way as you would for an advertised vacancy.

MYTH BUSTER
The role of an outplacement company is to find jobs for their clients

Wrong! This is not the role of an outplacement company. They provide career counselling services for many of their clients who have lost their job because of redundancy. This is particularly important for people who find that their negative feelings get in the way of their job search. They aim to empower their clients to carry out a positive job-search programme.

Corporate outplacement companies undertake work for companies and work to a code of practice. However, there are outplacement companies operating in the retail sector undertaking work for individual clients. A word of caution at this point – there's no code of practice for these companies, and their standards of service vary considerably.

REMEMBER
✓ The term 'hidden job market' refers to jobs that haven't been advertised, and therefore, generally speaking, aren't in the public domain. The hidden job market accounts for 80% of all vacancies.
✓ Accessing the hidden job market is about creating your own opportunities.
✓ The chances of getting a job from the hidden job market are considerably better than from the visible job market.
✓ Headhunters are in the business of executive search.
✓ Recruitment consultants specialise in advertising all vacancies on behalf of their clients.
✓ Employment agencies encourage applicants to register their career details so that they can be contacted when they have a suitable vacancy.
✓ Interim management is used by companies temporarily to fill a post whilst a permanent member of staff is being recruited.
✓ Networking is about meeting people formally or informally, on a one-to-one basis or in groups, and making the most of your contacts.

✓ Job searchers who send well-prepared speculative letters to employers often succeed in getting interviews and jobs.
✓ If your employer has paid for you to be provided with outplacement support, make full use of their vacancy information.

9 Conclusion

By now you should be aware of the steps to follow for finding jobs and securing interviews. You will have realised that job search is hard work. You need confidence and persistence to succeed, and an optimistic and positive approach to deal with the difficult times. There's no point in wasting valuable time worrying about rejection. The best way to deal with it is to move on and find other opportunities.

The time you've spent on self-assessment will prove to be invaluable for job-search and interview success. Again, it's worth repeating that this is a process that shouldn't be rushed. You will gain the confidence you need from an honest appraisal of your skills, personal strengths, weaknesses and values. Knowing yourself, and knowing what you want out of your next job, will be highly visible to any prospective employer.

One of your most challenging tasks is completing a CV. Keep in mind that this is your marketing tool and it should display the highest standard of content and presentation. Avoid slavishly following the examples in Chapter 5; they're there merely to help generate your own ideas. Instead, personalise your CV and include something in the content that's unique to you.

Job search is a serious business. It simply won't work if you see it as something that can be done in your spare time. Organising and planning your activities is essential, and will ensure that you still have time for yourself and your family.

Many readers are surprised to learn that the visible job market accounts for only 20% of the total available vacancies. Armed with this knowledge, you can allocate your time much more effectively between job sources in the visible and hidden job markets. In the visible job market, the Internet is growing at an incredible rate, and many more employers will use this to recruit their staff in the future. In the hidden job market, speculative approaches to employers and networking are the most successful job-search techniques. However, any serious job search should make use of as many of these job sources as possible.

This book is the first in the *Insider Guide* series. You will need *Career Networking* and *Interviews & Assessments*, by the same author, to complete the essential guide for all those who want to achieve career and job-search success in a changing workplace.

INTERNET RECRUITMENT

Search engines
www.excite.com
www.excite.co.uk
www.infoseek.com
www.lycos.com
www.lycos.co.uk
www.webcrawler.com
www.yahoo.com
www.yahoo.co.uk
www.god.co.uk
www.ukplus.co.uk

UK online recruitment websites
The Appointments Section – Offers a range of IT and telecommunications jobs.
Contact: **www.taps.com**

Job Hunter – Updated daily by the UK's regional press.
Contact: **www.jobhunter.co.uk**

Jobmail – Offers jobs in IT, education, engineering and the legal sector.
Contact: **www.jobmail.co.uk**

Jobserve – Claims to be the largest source of IT vacancies in the UK.
Contact: **www.jobserve.com/**

Jobs Go Public – Specialises in jobs in the public sector, charity and voluntary sectors.
Contact: **www.jobsgopublic.com**

Jobs in Food – Offers all types of jobs in catering.
Contact: **www.cateringnet.co.uk**

Jobs in UK Journalism – Specialises in vacancies for journalists looking for work in magazines and newspapers in the UK and worldwide.
Contact: **www.journalism.co.uk**

Jobsite – Offers a range of vacancies.
Contact: **www.jobsite.co.uk**

Marketing Week – Offers marketing jobs and articles appearing in the magazine.
Contact: **www.marketingweek.co.uk/index.htm/**

Netjobs – Offers a range of vacancies.
Contact: **www.netjobs.co.uk**

Personnel Health – Specialises in healthcare jobs.
Contact: **www.personnelnet.com/**

Prospects website – Association of Graduate Careers Advisory Services (AGCAS). For jobs and occupational information.
Contact: **www.prospects.csu.man.ac.uk**

Jobsunlimited – *The Guardian's* site.
Contact: **www.jobsunlimited.co.uk**

The Language Site – Offers jobs for specialists in translation work.
Contact: **www.interscript.com/**

The Monster Board – Offers a range of jobs.
Contact: **www.monster.co.uk**

Top Jobs on the Net – Offers a range of general positions.
Contact: **www.topjobs.net**

NEWSPAPERS

National newspaper job advertisements		
Newspaper	**Day of the week**	**Job sector**
Daily Mail	Tuesday	Clerical
		Secretarial
	Thursday	Clerical
		Engineering
		General Appointments
		Overseas
		Printing & Publishing
		Retail
		Sales
		Technical
Daily Telegraph	Thursday	Executive/Management
		General Appointments
The European	Wednesday	General Appointments in the European Community
The Express	Thursday	Catering/Hotel
		Engineering
		General Appointments
		Sales
		Technical
Financial Times	Wednesday	Banking
		Finance
		General Appointments
	Thursday	Accountancy
		Finance
The Guardian	Monday	Creative & Media
		Fund-raising
		Marketing
		PR
		Sales
		Secretarial
	Tuesday	Education
		General Appointments
	Wednesday	Environment
		Health
		Housing
		Public Sector
	Saturday	Careers
		Creative & Media
		Education

National newspaper job advertisements		
Newspaper	**Day of the week**	**Job sector**
The Guardian		General Appointments
		Graduates
		IT
		Marketing
		PR
The Independent	Tuesday	Public Sector
	Wednesday	Sales
		Science
		IT
		Accounting
		Banking
		Clerical
	Thursday	Finance
		Legal
The Independent on Sunday	Sunday	Office
Mail on Sunday	Sunday	Multilingual
The Observer	Sunday	Secretarial
		Education
		Graduates
		General Appointments
		All Sectors
		IT
Scotsman	Monday	General Appointments
	Tuesday	General Appointments
	Wednesday	General Appointments
		Education
	Thursday	General Appointments
		Public Sector
	Friday	General Appointments
		Marketing
		Sales
Sunday Telegraph	Sunday	Repeat of Thursday's Appointments Supplement
The Sunday Times	Sunday	All Sectors
The Times	Wednesday	Secretarial
	Thursday	Management
		Senior Appointments
		Secretarial
	Friday	Education
		Marketing
		Media
		Sales

A SELECTION OF OTHER PUBLICATIONS
CARRYING JOB ADVERTISEMENTS

Accountancy Age	Weekly
Architects' Journal	Weekly
Artists and Illustrators	Monthly
Banker, The	Monthly
British Journal of Photography	Weekly
British Medical Journal	Weekly
Building	Weekly
Caterer & Hotelkeeper	Weekly
Chemist & Druggist	Weekly
Community Care	Weekly
Education	Weekly
Engineering	Monthly
Farmers' Weekly	Weekly
Financial Advisor	Weekly
Grocer, The	Weekly
Housebuilder	Monthly
Insurance Age	Monthly
Lawyer, The	Weekly
Local Government Chronicle	Weekly
Marketing Week	Weekly
Media Week	Weekly
Money Marketing	Weekly
New Civil Engineer	Weekly
New Media Age	Weekly
Nursing Times & Nursing Mirror	Weekly
People Management	Bi-monthly
Printing World	Weekly
Retail Weekly	Weekly
Soap Perfumery & Cosmetics	Monthly
Sports Trader	Monthly
Surveyor	Weekly
Travel Trade Gazette	Weekly
Woodworker, The	Monthly

USEFUL ADDRESSES

Sources of career and industry information

Many of these organisations can provide you with useful career information or background to their industry. Send a letter setting out the information you require and for what purpose.

Administrative and clerical
Association of Medical Secretaries, Practice Administrators and Receptionists Ltd
Tavistock House North
Tavistock Square
London WC1H 9LN
Tel: 020 7387 6005

Advertising
The Advertising Association
Abford House
15 Wilton Road
London SW1V 1NJ
Tel: 020 7828 2771

Ambulance services
London Ambulance Service
The Recruitment Department
Central Division HQ
St Andrews House
St Andrews Way
Devons Road
London E3 3PA
Tel: 020 7887 6638

Animals
Animal Care College
Ascot House
29a High Street
Ascot
Berkshire SL5 7JG
Tel: 01344 628269

British Veterinary Nursing Association Ltd
Level 15
Terminus House
Terminus Street
Harlow
Essex CM20 1XA
Tel: 01279 450567

RSPCA
The Causeway
Horsham
West Sussex RH12 1HG
Tel: 0990 555999

Architecture
Architects and Surveying Institute
15 St Mary Street
Chippenham
Wiltshire SN15 3WD
Tel: 01249 444505

Art and design
Association of Illustrators
81 Leonard Street
London EC2A 4QS
Tel: 020 7613 4328

Chartered Society of Designers
1st Floor
32–38 Saffron Hill
London EC1N 8SG
Tel: 020 7831 9777

Banking
Chartered Institute of Bankers
4–9 Burgate Lane
Canterbury
Kent CT1 2XJ
Tel: 01227 762600

Beauty and hairdressing
Hairdressing and Beauty Industry Authority
Fraser House
Netherhall Road
Doncaster DN1 2PH
Tel: 01302 380000

National Hairdressers' Federation
11 Goldington Road
Bedford MK40 3JY
Tel: 01234 360332

Civil service
The Establishment Officer
Ordnance Survey
Romsey Road
Maybush
Southampton SO16 4GU
Tel: 02380 792000

Communications
Federation of Communications Services
Keswick House
207 Anerley Road
London SE20 8ER
Tel: 020 8778 5656

Computing
National Training Organisation for Information Technology
16–18 Berners Street
London W1P 3DD
Tel: 020 7580 6677

Construction
Construction Industry Training Board
Newton Training Centre
Bircham Newton
King's Lynn
Norfolk PE31 6RH
Tel: 01485 577577

Dentistry
British Dental Association
64 Wimpole Street
London WIM 8AL
Tel: 020 7935 0875

British Association of Dental Nurses
11 Pharos Street
Fleetwood
Lancashire FY7 6BG
Tel: 01253 778631

Engineering
Engineering Construction Industry Training Board
Blue Court
Church Lane
Kings Langley
Hertfordshire WD4 8JP
Tel: 01923 260000

The Engineering Careers Information Service
Enta House
14 Upton Road
Watford WD1 7EP
Tel: 0800 282167

Environment
Environment Agency
Public Enquiries Department
Rio House
Waterside Drive
Aztec West
Almondsbury
Bristol BS32 4UD
Tel: 01454 624400

English Nature
Enquiry Service
Room 1E
Northminster House
Peterborough PE1 1UA
Tel: 01733 455100

Finance

The Institute of Financial Accountants
Burford House
44 London Road
Sevenoaks
Kent TN13 1AS
Tel: 01732 458080

Chartered Institute of Management Accountants
63 Portland Place
London W1N 4AB
Tel: 020 7637 2311

Food and drink

Food and Drink National Training Organisation
Training Executive
6 Catherine Street
London WC2B 5JJ
Tel: 020 7836 2460

Gardening

Royal Horticultural Society
Supervisor of Studies and Training
Wisley
Woking
Surrey GU23 6QB
Tel: 01483 224234

The Institute of Horticulture
14–15 Belgrave Square
London SW1X 8PS
Tel: 020 7245 6943

Health service

NHS Careers
PO Box 376
Bristol BS99 3EY
Tel: 0845 6060655

Hotel and catering
Hotel, Catering and International Management Association
191 Trinity Road
London SW17 7HN
Tel: 020 8672 4251

Human resources and personnel
Institute of Personnel and Development
Camp Road
Wimbledon
London SW19 4UX
Tel: 020 8971 9000

Insurance
The Chartered Insurance Institute
20 Aldermanbury
London EC2V 7HY
Tel: 020 7417 4793

Languages
The Institute of Linguists
Saxon House
48 Southwark Street
London SE1 1UN
Tel: 020 7940 3100

Law
The Law Society
Legal Education Information Unit
Ipsley Court
Berrington Close
Redditch
Worcestershire B98 0TD
Tel: 01527 517141

Crown Prosecution Service
Recruitment Branch
50 Ludgate Hill
London EC4M 7EX
Tel: 020 7796 8000

Institute of Legal Executives
Kempston Manor
Kempston
Bedfordshire MK42 7AB
Tel: 01234 841000

Library work
The Library Association
7 Ridgmount Street
London WC1E 7AE
Tel: 020 7255 0500

Management
Institute of Management
Management House
Cottingham Road
Corby
Northants NN17 1TT
Tel: 01536 204222

Marketing
The Chartered Institute of Marketing
Moor Hall
Cookham
Maidenhead
Berkshire SL6 9QH
Tel: 01628 427310

Market research
The Market Research Society
15 Northburgh Street
London EC1V 0JR
Tel: 020 7490 4911

The media
National Council for the Training of Journalists
The Latton Bush Centre
Southern Way
Harlow
Essex CM18 7BL
Tel: 01279 430009

Medical and nursing
British Medical Association
BMA House
Tavistock Square
London WC1H 9JP
Tel: 020 7387 4499

Royal College of Nursing
20 Cavendish Square
London W1M 0AB
Tel: 020 7409 3333

Pharmacy
The Royal Pharmaceutical Society of Great Britain
1 Lambeth High Street
London SE1 7JN
Tel: 020 7735 9141

Photography
Association of Photographers
31 Leonard Street
London EC2A 4QS
Tel: 020 7739 6669

Physiotherapy
The Chartered Society of Physiotherapy
14 Bedford Row
London WC1R 4ED
Tel: 020 7306 6666

Publishing and bookselling
The Publishers Association
1 Kingsway
London WC2B 6XO
Tel: 020 7565 7474

Booksellers Association of Great Britain
272 Vauxhall Bridge Road
London SW1V 1BA
Tel: 020 7834 5477

Sport

Sport England
16 Upper Woburn Place
London WC1H 0QP
Tel: 020 7273 1500

Sports Council for Northern Ireland
House of Sport
Upper Malone Road
Belfast BT9 5LA
Tel: 02890 381222

Sport Scotland
Caledonia House
South Gyle
Edinburgh EH12 9DQ
Tel: 0131 317 7200

The Sports Council for Wales
Sophia Gardens
Cardiff CF11 9SW
Tel: 029 2030 0500

Teaching

Teaching Training Agency
Portland House
Stag Place
London SW1E 5TT
Tel: 020 7925 3700

Travel and tourism

Institute of Travel and Tourism
113 Victoria Street
St Albans
Hertfordshire AL1 3TJ
Tel: 01727 854395

Interim management

Albemarle Interim Management Services
26–28 Great Portland Street
London WIN 5AD
Tel: 020 7631 1991

Ernst & Young Corporate Resources
Roll House
7 Rolls Buildings
Fetter Lane
London EC4A 1NH
Tel: 020 7951 2000

Executive Interim Management
39 St James' Street
London SW1A 1JD
Tel: 020 7290 1430

PA Consulting Group
123 Buckingham Palace Road
London SW1W 9SR
Tel: 020 7730 9000

Russam GMS Ltd
48 High Street North
Dunstable
Bedfordshire LU6 1LA
Tel: 01582 666970

Training and education

Information and advice can be obtained from the following:

Career Development Loans
Freepost
PO Box 354
Warrington WA4 6XU
Tel: 0800 585505

ECCTIS 2000
Oriel House
Oriel Road
Cheltenham
Gloucestershire GL50 IXP
Tel: 01242 252627

The Industrial Society
Robert Hyde House
48 Bryanston Square
London WIH 2EA
Tel: 020 7479 2000

Institute of Management
Management House
Cottingham Road
Corby
Northants NN17 ITT
Tel: 01536 204222

Institute of Personnel and Development
35 Camp Road
Wimbledon
London SW19 4UX
Tel: 020 8971 9000

Local Education Authorities (look in your local *Yellow Pages*)

National Extension College
18 Brooklands Avenue
Cambridge
CB2 2HN
Tel: 01223 450200

Open University
Admissions Office
PO Box 46
Milton Keynes MK7 6AP
Tel: 01908 274066

Royal Society of Arts
6 John Adam Street
London WC2N 6EZ
Tel: 020 7930 5115

FURTHER READING

Headhunters and recruitment consultants

The Executive Grapevine, published by Executive Grapevine International.

CEPEC Recruitment Guide, published by CEPEC Ltd.

The Personnel Manager's Yearbook, published by A. P. Information Services.

Yearbook of Recruitment and Employment Services, published by A. P. Information Services.

CAREER PUBLICATIONS FROM THE INDUSTRIAL SOCIETY

The Insider Guides
Job Search
Brian Sutton
ISBN 1 85835 815 9

Career Networking
Brian Sutton
ISBN 1 85835 825 6

Interviews & Assessments
Brian Sutton
ISBN 1 85835 820 5

The Insider Career Guides

Advertising, Marketing & PR
Karen Holmes
ISBN 1 85835 872 8

Banking & the City
Karen Holmes
ISBN 1 85835 583 4

Broadcasting & the Media
Paul Redstone
ISBN 1 85835 867 1

The Environment
Melanie Allen
ISBN 1 85835 588 5

Information & Communications Technology
Jacquetta Megarry
ISBN 1 85835 593 1

Retailing
Liz Edwards
ISBN 1 85835 578 8

Sport
Robin Hardwick
ISBN 1 85835 573 7

Travel & Tourism
Karen France
ISBN 1 85835 598 2